MORE
to
YOUR
STORY

ALSO BY MAX LUCADO

MORE
to
YOUR STORY

DISCOVER YOUR PLACE IN GOD'S PLAN

MAX LUCADO

THOMAS NELSON
Since 1798

ISBN 978-0-7180-3133-6
ISBN 978-0-7180-3551-8 (eBook)

God's Story, Your Story editions:
ISBN 978-0-3102-9403-0 (HC)
ISBN 978-0-3108-8987-8 (Participant's Guide)
ASIN 025986889869 (DVD)

The Library of Congress has cataloged an earlier edition as follows:

Lucado, Max.
God's story, your story : when His becomes yours / Max Lucado.
p. cm.
Includes bibliographical references.
ISBN 978-0-310-29403-0 (hardcover, jacketed)
1. Christian life. I. Title.
BV4501.3.L826 2011
248.4—dc22   2011006758

Printed in the United States of America

16 17 18 19 20 RRD 10 9 8 7 6 5 4 3 2 1

Denalyn and I happily dedicate this book
to my sister and brother-in-law
Joan and Fred Carrigan.
You've brought joy and laughter
to every page of our story,
and we love you!

GOD rewrote the text of my life
    when I opened the book of my heart to his eyes.

2 SAMUEL 22:25 MSG

CONTENTS

ACKNOWLEDGMENTS

Quite a cast made this production possible! Each one is worthy of a loud ovation:

Liz Heaney and Karen Hill monitored each sentence and helped me polish each paragraph. I deeply appreciate you both.

Carol Bartley applied her one-of-a-kind, sleuth-level copyediting. I am indebted to you.

Randy and Rozanne Frazee — I'm so grateful for the idea, even more grateful for the partnership.

Dudley Delffs oversaw every stage of creation and production. Great work, friend.

Byron Williamson and Steve and Cheryl Green managed to resuscitate this book more than once. Without you, who knows what would have happened?

Moe Girkins and the outstanding team at Zondervan elevated The Story initiative to a higher level. I am proud to work with you!

David Drury added his always-valuable theological insights.

Brad Tuggle offered valuable suggestions.

David Treat covered this book and the team in prayer.

My family: Brett and Jenna Bishop, Andrea and Sara Lucado. You teach me more about God's love than you will ever know.

My wife, Denalyn. God gave me you *and* heaven. Is it possible to be blessed too much? If so, I qualify. I love you!

INTRODUCTION

When You Discover Your Place in God's Plan ...

Ralls, Texas, was a weathered tumbleweed of a town in 1965. The city center consisted of a two-story courthouse framed by a weedy lawn and bricked roads. One drugstore had gone out of business; the second was not far behind. The shelves of the five-and-dime were dusty and empty, like the street upon which it sat. The closest facsimile of a traffic jam occurred every morning when the farmers left the diner parking lot after their sunrise coffee.

Someone had pressed the pause button and forgotten to release it.

Which was just fine with my grandparents, God bless 'em. Charles and Macey McDermott looked just like the farm couple in Grant Wood's painting, only not nearly as energetic. Grandpa, lanky and long faced; she, shorter and dark eyed. Neither one smiled much. They shuffled about in a two-bedroom frame house, chewing Brown's Mule tobacco, watching soap operas, and reading Zane Grey novels.

It was my mom's idea for me to spend a week with them. Let ten-year-old Max get to know his grandparents' and mom's hometown. So she gave me a chocolate bar and a kiss, loaded me on a Greyhound bus, and waved good-bye. The trip peaked with the candy bar. After one day I knew this was going to be the longest week of my life. My grandparents had no bicycles, baseballs, or basketball hoops. They knew no other ten-year-olds and lived too far out in the country for me to find any. Dullsville. I would have accepted an invitation to watch paint dry.

But then came the story.

Over lunch one day I asked my grandmother about the photo that hung in her bedroom: the sepia-toned picture that was professionally taken and handsomely set in an oval-shaped walnut frame. Who was this mystery man who occupied prime real estate above my grandmother's side of the bed? He stood next to a chair, one hand on its back and the other holding a fedora. His slender face came to a point at his nose. His forehead was whiter than the rest of his face, his hair slicked straight back, black and shiny, as if coated with engine grease. He was stiff and rigid, clearly uncomfortable in the three-piece suit and photography studio.

"That's Levi Thornton," Grandma told me, "your mother's first father. Your grandfather." I'd heard of this man. How he brought my mom to the farm country. How he died young. But where he came from? How he died? I didn't know.

So Grandma set out to tell me. Within a couple of sentences, I was lost in the story, bouncing in the cab of the 1929 Chevy pickup with Grandpa Levi, Grandma, and an eight-year-old version of my mom. They were migrating to the Texas Panhandle from Cherokee, Oklahoma, in search of an affordable farm and fertile soil. They found both. But then a drought took the crop, and tuberculosis took Levi's health. Macey drove the truck back to Cherokee, where Levi died in her arms. He was buried at the age of thirty-three.

Grandma's telling lasted more than a paragraph, of course, given that I was happy to listen and she was thrilled to talk. We shinnied up the family tree and spent the better part of the day exploring branches I had never known existed. As we did, my black-and-white week exploded into a Monet of colors.

Why do you suppose, now forty years removed, I

remember the day in such detail? I still see the kitchen in which we sat, its straight-backed chairs and Formica-topped table. I see Grandma spilling photos out of a box and details out of her heart as if neither had been taken off the shelf in quite some time. I recall an emotion akin to the one you felt when you learned about your great-grandfather's migration from Norway or a distant relation being one of the charter Royal Canadian Mounties. Perhaps you've traced your ancestry through the Apache's hunting grounds, African slave ships, or Polynesian sailors. We love to know where we came from.

We *need* to know where we came from. Knowing connects us, links us, bonds us to something greater than we are. Knowing reminds us that we aren't floating on isolated ponds but on a grand river.

That's why God wants you to know his story. Framed photos hang in his house. Lively talks await you at his table. A scrapbook sits in his living room, brimming with stories. Stories about Bethlehem beginnings and manger miracles. Enemy warfare in the wilderness and fishermen friends in Galilee. The stumbles of Peter, the stubbornness of Paul. All a part of the story.

But they are all subplots to the central message: "For God so loved the world that he gave his one and only Son, that whoever believes in him shall not perish but have eternal life" (John 3:16). This is the headline of the story: God saves his people! He casts his net over cities and individuals, princes and paupers, the Pontius Pilates of power and the Peters, Jameses, and Johns of the fishing villages. God takes on the whole mess of us and cleans us up.

This quest is God's story. And we are a part of it!

We can easily miss this. Life keeps pulling us down. The traffic, the troubles. The doctor visits and home-work. Life is Ralls, Texas, and nothing more. No prelude or sequel. Just tumbleweeds and dust and birth and death. And the randomness of it all. One week you are hav-ing a baby; the next you are having to move out of your house. "Good news, a bonus!" "Bad news, a blizzard." Hec-tic. Haphazard. Playgrounds and cemeteries on the same block.

Is there a story line to this drama?

I asked the same question. About the same time I traveled to Ralls, I received another invitation. The local community theater group was staging the play *The Wizard of Oz*, and they needed some Munchkins. They recruited the children's choir (in which I sang second soprano, thank you very much) to play the parts. We learned the songs and practiced the dances, but our choir direc-tor overlooked one detail. He never told us the story. He assumed we'd seen the movie. I hadn't. As far as I knew, Toto was a chocolate candy, and the Yellow Brick Road was an avenue in Disneyland. I knew nothing of Kansas tornadoes or hot-air balloons. I didn't know how the story started or ended, but I found myself in the middle of it.

Dress rehearsal nearly did me in. A house crashed out of the sky. A queen floated in a bubble. A long-nosed witch waved her stick. "I'll get you, my pretty . . ." I was wide-eyed and wondering what I'd gotten myself into. Life in Munchkinland can be a scary thing.

Unless you've read the screenplay. Unless you know the final act. When you enter the stage equipped with a script, everything changes. You know that in the end the witch melts. So let her cackle all she wants; her days are numbered. In the end, good wins.

Everything changes when you know the rest of your story.

As David discovered, "GOD rewrote the text of my life when I opened the book of my heart to his eyes" (2 Samuel 22:25 MSG). But what is the text of our lives?

The question is not a new one. Self-help gurus, talk-show hosts, and magazine headlines urge you to find your narrative. But they send you in the wrong direction. "Look inside yourself," they say. But the promise of self-discovery falls short. Can you find the plot of a book in one paragraph or hear the flow of a symphony in one measure? Can you uncover the plot of your life by examining your life? By no means. You are so much more than a few days between the womb and the tomb.

Your story indwells God's. This is the great promise of the Bible and the hope of this book. "It's in Christ that we find out who we are and what we are living for. Long before we first heard of Christ and got our hopes up, he had his eye on us, had designs on us for glorious living, part of the overall purpose he is working out in everything and everyone" (Ephesians 1:11–12 MSG).

Above and around us God directs a grander saga, written by his hand, orchestrated by his will, unveiled according to his calendar. And you are a part of it. Meaningless Munchkin? Not you. Stranded on the prairie in a creaky old farmhouse? No way. Your life emerges from the greatest mind and the kindest heart in the history of the universe: the mind and heart of God. "He makes everything work out according to his plan" (Ephesians 1:11 NLT).

Let's dive into his story, shall we? Our plan is simple: journey though the New Testament in search of God's narrative. We'll use the chronological Bible *The Story* as our guidebook, extracting a promise from each of its ten chapters.

Who knows? In his story we might find our own.

CHAPTER ONE

When You Discover Your Place in God's Plan ...

ORDINARY MATTERS

THE PINT-SIZE JOSEPH SCURRIES ACROSS THE CHURCH
stage, wearing sandals, a robe, and his best attempt at an
anxious face. He raps on the door his dad built for the
children's Christmas play, then shifts from one foot to the
other, partly because he's supposed to act nervous. Mostly
because he is exactly that.

The innkeeper answers. He too wears a tow sack of a
robe and a towel turned turban. An elastic band secures
a false beard to his face. He looks at Joseph and chokes
back a giggle. Just a couple of hours ago the two boys were
building a front-lawn snowman. Their moms had to tell
them twice to get dressed for the Christmas Eve service.

Here they stand. The innkeeper crosses his arms;
Joseph waves his. He describes a donkey ride from

Nazareth, five days on the open road, a census here in Bethlehem, and, most of all, a wife. He turns and points in the direction of a pillow-stuffed nine-year-old girl.

She waddles onto center stage with one hand on the small of her back and the other mopping her brow. She limps with her best portrayal of pregnant pain, though, if pressed, she would have no clue about the process of childbirth.

She plays up the part. Groan. Sigh. "Joseph, I need help!"

The crowd chuckles.

Joseph looks at the innkeeper.

The innkeeper looks at Mary.

And we all know what happens next. Joseph urges. The innkeeper shakes his head. His hotel is packed. Guests occupy every corner. There is no room at the inn.

I think some dramatic license could be taken here. Rather than hurry to the next scene, let Joseph plead his case. "Mr. Innkeeper, think twice about your decision. Do you know whom you are turning away? That's God inside that girl! You're closing the door on the King of the universe. Better reconsider. Do you really want to be memorialized as the person who turned out heaven's child into the cold?"

And let the innkeeper react. "I've heard some desperate appeals for a room, but *God inside a girl?* That girl? She has pimples and puffy ankles, for goodness' sake! Doesn't look like a God-mother to me. And you don't look too special yourself there ... uh ... What was your name? Oh yeah, Joe. Good ol' Joe. Covered head to toe with road dust. Take your tale somewhere else, buddy. I'm not falling for your story. Sleep in the barn for all I care!"

The innkeeper huffs and turns. Joseph and Mary exit. The choir sings "Away in a Manger" as stagehands wheel out a pile of hay, a feed trough, and some plastic sheep. The audience smiles and claps and sings along. They love the song, the kids, and they cherish the story. But most of all, they cling to the hope. The Christmas hope that God indwells the everydayness of our world.

The story drips with normalcy. This isn't *Queen* Mary or *King* Joseph. The couple doesn't caravan into Bethlehem with camels, servants, purple banners, and dancers. Mary and Joseph have no tax exemption or political connection. They have the clout of a migrant worker and the net worth of a minimum wage earner.

Not subjects for a PBS documentary.

Not candidates for welfare either. Their life is difficult but not destitute. Joseph has the means to pay taxes. They inhabit the populous world between royalty and rubes.

They are, well, normal. Normal has calluses like

Joseph, stretch marks like Mary. Normal stays up late with laundry and wakes up early for work. Normal drives the car pool wearing a bathrobe and slippers. Normal is Norm and Norma, not Prince and Princess.

Norm sings off-key. Norma works in a cubicle and struggles to find time to pray. Both have stood where Joseph stood and have heard what Mary heard. Not from the innkeeper in Bethlehem, but from the coach in middle school or the hunk in high school or the foreman at the plant. "We don't have room for you … time for you … a space for you … a job for you … interest in you. Besides, look at you. You are too slow … fat … inexperienced … late … young … old … pigeon-toed … cross-eyed … hackneyed. You are too … ordinary."

But then comes the Christmas story — Norm and Norma from Normal, Ohio, plodding into ho-hum Bethlehem in the middle of the night. No one notices them. No one looks twice in their direction. The innkeeper won't even clean out a corner in the attic. Trumpets don't blast; bells don't sound; angels don't toss confetti. Aren't we glad they didn't?

What if Joseph and Mary had shown up in furs with a chauffeur, bling-blinged and high-muckety-mucked? And what if God had decked out Bethlehem like Hollywood on Oscar night: red carpet, flashing lights, with angels interviewing the royal couple? "Mary, Mary, you look simply divine."

Had Jesus come with such whoop-de-do, we would have read the story and thought, My, *look how Jesus entered their world.*

But since he didn't, we can read the story and dream. My, *might Jesus be born in my world? My everyday world?*

Isn't that what you indwell? Not a holiday world. Or a red-letter-day world. No, you live an everyday life. You have bills to pay, beds to make, and grass to cut. Your face won't grace any magazine covers, and you aren't expecting a call from the White House. Congratulations. You qualify for a modern-day Christmas story. God enters the world through folks like you and comes on days like today.

The splendor of the first Christmas is the lack thereof.

Step into the stable, and cradle in your arms the infant Jesus, still moist from the womb, just wrapped in the rags. Run a finger across his chubby cheek, and listen as one who knew him well puts lyrics to the event:

"In the beginning was the Word" (John 1:1).

The words "In the beginning" take us to the beginning. "In the beginning God created the heavens and the earth" (Genesis 1:1). The baby Mary held was connected to the dawn of time. He saw the first ray of sunlight and heard the first crash of a wave. The baby was born, but the Word never was.

"All things were made through him" (1 Corinthians 8:6 NCV). Not *by* him, but *through* him. Jesus didn't fashion the world out of raw material he found. He created all things out of nothing.

Jesus: the Genesis Word, "the firstborn over all creation" (Colossians 1:15). He is the "one Lord, Jesus Christ, through whom God made everything and through whom we have been given life" (1 Corinthians 8:6 NLT).

And then, what no theologian conceived, what no rabbi dared to dream, God did. "The Word became flesh" (John 1:14). The Artist became oil on his own palette. The Potter melted into the mud on his own wheel. God became an embryo in the belly of a village girl. Christ in Mary. God in Christ.

Astounding, this thought of heaven's fetus floating within the womb. Joseph and Mary didn't have the advantage we have: ultrasound. When Denalyn was pregnant with each of our three daughters, we took full advantage of the technology. The black-and-white image on the screen looked more like Doppler radar than a child. But with the help of the doctor, we were able to see the arms and hands and the pierced nose and prom dress ... Wait, I'm confusing photos.

As the doctor moved the instrument around Dena-lyn's belly, he took inventory. "There's the head, the feet, the torso ... Well, everything looks normal."

Mary's doctor would have made the same announce-ment. Jesus was an ordinary baby. There is nothing in the story to imply that he levitated over the manger or walked out of the stable. Just the opposite. He "dwelt among us" (John 1:14 NKJV). John's word for *dwelt* traces its origin to *tabernacle* or *tent*. Jesus did not separate himself from his creation; he pitched his tent in the neighborhood.

The Word of God entered the world with the cry of a baby. His family had no cash or connections or strings to pull. Jesus, the Maker of the universe, the one who invented time and created breath, was born into a family too humble to swing a bed for a pregnant mom-to-be.

❖

God writes his story with people like Joseph and Mary ... and Sam Stone.

In the weeks before Christmas 1933, a curious offer appeared in the daily newspaper of Canton, Ohio. "Man Who Felt Depression's Sting to Help 75 Unfortunate

Families." A Mr. B. Virdot promised to send a check to the neediest in the community. All they had to do was describe their plight in a letter and mail it to General Delivery.

The plunging economy had left fathers with no jobs, houses with no heat, children with patched clothing, and an entire nation, it seemed, with no hope.

The appeals poured in.

"I hate to write this letter ... it seems too much like begging ... my husband doesn't know I'm writing ... He is working but not making enough to hardly feed his family."

"Mr. Virdot, we are in desperate circumstances ... No one knows, only those who go through it."

All of Canton knew of Mr. Virdot's offer. Oddly, no one knew Mr. Virdot. The city registry of 105,000 citizens contained no such name. People wondered if he really existed. Yet within a week checks began to arrive at homes all over the area. Most were modest, about five dollars. All were signed "B. Virdot."

Through the years, the story was told, but the identity of the man was never discovered. In 2008, long after his death, a grandson opened a tattered black suitcase that had collected dust in his parents' attic. That's where he found the letters, all dated in December 1933, as well as 150 canceled checks. Mr. B. Virdot was Samuel J. Stone.

His pseudonym was a hybrid of Barbara, Virginia, and Dorothy, the names of his three daughters.[1]

There was nothing privileged about Sam Stone. If anything, his upbringing was marred by challenge. He was fifteen when his family emigrated from Romania. They settled into a Pittsburgh ghetto, where his father hid Sam's shoes so he couldn't go to school and forced him and his six siblings to roll cigars in the attic.

Still, Stone persisted. He left home to work on a barge, then in a coal mine, and by the time the Depression hit, he owned a small chain of clothing stores and lived in relative comfort. He wasn't affluent, or impoverished, but he was willing to help.

Ordinary man. Ordinary place. But a conduit of extraordinary grace. And in God's story, ordinary matters.

CHAPTER TWO

When You Discover Your Place in God's Plan ...

YOU KNOW SATAN'S NEXT MOVE

IF I WERE THE DEVIL, I'D BE TICKED OFF. TICKED OFF TO SEE you reading a Christian book, thinking godly thoughts, dreaming about heaven and other such blah-blah-blah.

How dare you ponder God's story! What about my story? I had my eyes on you . . . had plans for you. That's what I would think.

If I were the devil, I'd get busy. I'd assemble my minions and demons into a strategy session and give them your picture and address. I'd review your weaknesses one by one. *Don't think I don't know them. How you love to be liked and hate to be wrong. How cemeteries give you the creeps and darkness gives you the heebie-jeebies.*

I'd brief my staff on my past victories. *Haven't I had my share? Remember your bouts with doubt? I all but had you convinced that the Bible was a joke. You and your so-called faith in God's Word.*

I'd stealth my way into your mind. No frontal attacks for you. Witchcraft and warlocks won't work with your type. No. If I were the devil, I'd dismantle you with questions. *How do you know, I mean, truly know, that Jesus rose from the dead? Are you sure you* really *believe the gospel? Isn't absolute truth yesterday's news? You, a child of God? Come on.*

I might direct you to one of my churches. One of my "feel good, you're good, everything's good" churches. Half Hollywood, half pep talk. Glitz, lights, and love. But no talk of Jesus. No mention of sin, hell, or forgiveness. I'd asphyxiate you with promises of pay raises and new cars. Then again, you're a bit savvy for that strategy.

Distraction would work better. *I hate spiritual focus. When you or one like you gazes intently on God for any length of time, you begin to act like him. A nauseating sense of justice and virtue comes over you. You talk to God, not just once a week, but all the time. Intolerable.*

So I'd perch myself on every corner and stairwell of your world, clamoring for your attention. I'd flood you with e-mails and to-do lists. Entice you with shopping sprees and latest releases and newest styles. Burden you with deadlines and assignments.

If I were the devil, I'd so distract you with possessions and problems that you'd never have time to read the Bible. Especially the story of Jesus in the wilderness. *What a disaster that day was! Jesus brought me down. Coldcocked me. Slam-dunked one right over my head. He knocked my best pitch over the Green Monster. I never even landed a punch. Looking back, I now realize what he was doing. He was making a statement. He wanted the whole world to know who calls the shots in the universe.*

If I were the devil, I wouldn't want you to read about that encounter. So, for that reason alone, let's do.

Then Jesus was led by the Spirit into the wilderness to be tempted by the devil. After fasting forty days and forty nights, he was hungry. The tempter came to him and said, "If you are the Son of God, tell these stones to become bread."

Jesus answered, "It is written: 'Man shall not live on bread alone, but on every word that comes from the mouth of God.'"

Then the devil took him to the holy city and had him stand on the highest point of the temple. "If you are the Son of God," he said, "throw yourself down. For it is written:

"'He will command his angels concerning you,

and they will lift you up in their hands,
so that you will not strike your foot against
a stone.'"

Jesus answered him, "It is also written: 'Do not put the Lord your God to the test.'"

Again, the devil took him to a very high mountain and showed him all the kingdoms of the world and their splendor. "All this I will give you," he said, "if you will bow down and worship me."

Jesus said to him, "Away from me, Satan! For it is written: 'Worship the Lord your God, and serve him only.'"

Then the devil left him, and angels came and attended him.

MATTHEW 4:1–11

Jesus was fresh out of the Jordan River. He had just been baptized by John. At his baptism he had been affirmed by God with a dove and a voice: "You are my Son, whom I love; with you I am well pleased" (Luke 3:22). He stepped out of the waters buoyed by God's blessing. Yet he began his public ministry, not by healing the sick or preaching a sermon, but by exposing the scheme of Satan. A perfect place to begin.

How do we explain our badness? Our stubborn hearts

and hurtful hands and conniving ways? How do we explain Auschwitz, human trafficking, abuse? Trace malevolence upriver to its beginning, where will the river take us? What will we see?

If I were the devil, I'd blame evil on a broken political system. A crippled economy. The roll of the dice. The Wicked Witch of the West. I'd want you to feel attacked by an indefinable, nebulous force. After all, if you can't diagnose the source of your ills, how can you treat them? If I were the devil, I'd keep my name out of it.

But God doesn't let the devil get away with this and tells us his name. The Greek word for devil is *diabolos*, which shares a root with the verb *diaballein*, which means "to split." The devil is a splitter, a divider, a wedge driver. He divided Adam and Eve from God in the garden, and has every intent of doing the same to you. Blame all unrest on him. Don't fault the plunging economy or raging dictator for your anxiety. They are simply tools in Satan's tool kit. He is the

- serpent (Genesis 3:14; Revelation 12:9; 20:2)

- tempter (Matthew 4:3; 1 Thessalonians 3:5)

- enemy (Matthew 13:25, 39)

- evil one (Matthew 13:19; 1 John 2:13–14)

43

- prince of demons (Mark 3:22)

- father of lies (John 8:44)

- murderer (John 8:44)

- roaring lion (1 Peter 5:8)

- deceiver (Revelation 12:9 GWT)

- dragon (Revelation 12:7, 9; 20:2)

Satan is not absent from or peripheral to God's story. He is at its center. We can't understand God's narrative without understanding Satan's strategy. In fact, "the reason the Son of God appeared was to destroy the works of the devil" (1 John 3:8 ESV).

Nothing thrills Satan more than the current skepticism with which he is viewed. When people deny his existence or chalk up his works to the ills of society, he rubs his hands with glee. The more we doubt his very existence, the more he can work without hindrance.

Jesus didn't doubt the reality of the devil. The Savior strode into the badlands with one goal, to unmask Satan, and made him the first stop on his itinerary. "Then Jesus was led by the Spirit into the wilderness to be tempted by the devil" (Matthew 4:1).

Does God do the same with us? Might the Spirit of

God lead us into the wilderness? If I were the devil, I'd tell you no. I would want you to think that I, on occasion, snooker heaven. That I catch God napping. That I sneak in when he isn't looking and snatch his children out of his hand. I'd leave you sleeping with one eye open.

But Scripture reveals otherwise. The next time you hear the phrase "all hell broke loose," correct the speaker. Hell does not break loose. God uses Satan's temptation to strengthen us. (If I were the devil, that would aggravate me to no end.) Times of testing are actually times of training, purification, and strength building. You can even "consider it pure joy … whenever you face trials of many kinds, because you know that the testing of your faith produces perseverance" (James 1:2–3).

God loves you too much to leave you undeveloped and immature. "God disciplines us for our good, that we may share in his holiness. No discipline seems pleasant at the time, but painful. Later on, however, it produces a harvest of righteousness and peace for those who have been trained by it" (Hebrews 12:10–11). Expect to be tested by the devil.

And watch for his tricks. You can know what to expect. "We are not ignorant of his schemes" (2 Corinthians 2:11 NASB).

When General George Patton counterattacked Field

Marshal Rommel in World War II, Patton is reported to have shouted in the thick of battle, "I read your book, Rommel! I read your book!" Patton had studied Rommel's *Infantry Attacks*. He knew the German leader's strategy and planned his moves accordingly.[2] We can know the same about the devil.

We know Satan will *attack weak spots first*. Forty days of fasting left Jesus famished, so Satan began with the topic of bread. Jesus' stomach was empty, so to the stomach Satan turned.

Where are you empty? Are you hungry for attention, craving success, longing for intimacy? Be aware of your weaknesses. Bring them to God before Satan brings them to you. Satan will tell you to turn stones into bread (Matthew 4:3). In other words, *meet your own needs*, take matters into your own hands, leave God out of the picture. Whereas Jesus teaches us to pray for bread (Matthew 6:11), Satan says to work for bread.

Besides, he said, "If you are the Son of God" (Matthew 4:3), you can do this. Ah, another ploy: *raise a question about identity*. Make Christians think they have to prove their position with rock-to-bread miracles. Clever. If Satan convinces us to trust our works over God's Word, he has us dangling from a broken limb. Our works will never hold us.

Jesus didn't even sniff the bait. Three times he repeated, "It is written …"; "It is also written …"; "it is written …" (verses 4, 7, 10). In his book, God's book was enough. He overcame temptation, not with special voices or supernatural signs, but by remembering and quoting Scripture.

(If I were the devil, I wouldn't want you to underline that sentence.)

Satan regrouped and tried a different approach. This one may surprise you. He told Jesus to *show off in church.* "Then the devil took him to the holy city and had him stand on the highest point of the temple. 'If you are the Son of God,' he said, 'throw yourself down'" (verses 5–6).

Testing isn't limited to the desert; it also occurs in the sanctuary. The two stood on the southeastern wall of the temple, more than a hundred feet above the Kidron Valley, and Satan told Jesus to jump into the arms of God. Jesus refused, not because he couldn't, not because God wouldn't catch him. He refused because he didn't have to prove anything to anyone, much less the devil.

Neither do you. Satan is going to tell you otherwise. In church, of all places, he will urge you to do tricks: impress others with your service, make a show of your faith, call attention to your good deeds. He loves to turn church assemblies into Las Vegas presentations where people show off their abilities rather than boast in God's. Don't be suckered.

Satan's last shot began with a mountain climb. "The devil took him to a very high mountain" (verse 8). Another note out of Satan's playbook: *promise heights*. Promise the highest place, the first place, the peak, the pinnacle. The best, the most, the top. These are Satan's favorite words. The devil led Jesus higher and higher, hoping, I suppose, that the thin air would confuse his thinking. He "showed [Jesus] all the kingdoms of the world and their splendor. 'All this I will give you,' he said, 'if you will bow down and worship me'" (verses 8–9).

Oops. Satan just showed his cards. He wants worship. He wants you and me to tell him how great he is. He wants to write his own story in which he is the hero and God is an afterthought. He admitted as much:

> "I will ascend to the heavens;
> I will raise my throne
>   above the stars of God;
> I will sit enthroned on the mount of assembly,
>   on the utmost heights of Mount Zaphon.
> I will ascend above the tops of the clouds;
>   I will make myself like the Most High."
>
> ISAIAH 14:13–14

Satan wants to take God's place, but God isn't moving. Satan covets the throne of heaven, but God isn't leaving. Satan wants to win you to his side, but God will never let you go.

You have his word. Even more, you have God's help.

> For our high priest [Jesus] is able to understand our weaknesses. When he lived on earth, he was tempted in every way that we are, but he did not sin. Let us, then, feel very sure that we can come before God's throne where there is grace. There we can receive mercy and grace to help us when we need it.
>
> HEBREWS 4:15–16 NCV

The last two Greek words of that verse are *eukairon boētheian*. *Eukairos* means "timely" or "seasonable" or "opportune." *Boētheia* is a compound of *boē*, "to shout," and *theō*, "to run." Nice combination. We shout, and God runs at the right moment. God places himself prior to our need, and just before we encounter that need, he gives us what we need.

You don't have to face Satan alone. You know his schemes. He will attack your weak spots first. He will tell you to meet your own needs. When you question your identity as a child of God, that is Satan speaking. If you turn church into a talent show, now you know why.

Even more, now you know what to do.

Pray. We cannot do battle with Satan on our own. He is a roaring lion, a fallen angel, an experienced fighter, and an equipped soldier. He is angry—angry because he knows that his time is short (Revelation 12:12) and that God's victory is secure. He resents God's goodness toward us and our worship of God. He is a skillful, powerful, ruthless foe who seeks to "work us woe; His craft and power are great, and armed with cruel hate, on earth is not his equal."[3] But there is wonderful news for the Christian: Christ reigns as our protector and provider. We are more than conquerors through him (Romans 8:37).

Arm yourself with God's Word. Load your pistol with Scriptures and keep a finger on the trigger. And remember: "Our struggle is not against flesh and blood, but against the rulers, against the authorities, against the powers of this dark world and against the spiritual forces of evil in the heavenly realms" (Ephesians 6:12).

If I were the devil, I wouldn't want you to know that. But I'm not the devil, so good for you. And take that, Satan.

CHAPTER THREE

When You Discover Your Place in God's Plan ...

YOU FIND
YOUR TRUE HOME

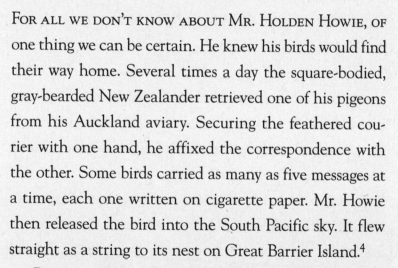

FOR ALL WE DON'T KNOW ABOUT MR. HOLDEN HOWIE, OF one thing we can be certain. He knew his birds would find their way home. Several times a day the square-bodied, gray-bearded New Zealander retrieved one of his pigeons from his Auckland aviary. Securing the feathered courier with one hand, he affixed the correspondence with the other. Some birds carried as many as five messages at a time, each one written on cigarette paper. Mr. Howie then released the bird into the South Pacific sky. It flew straight as a string to its nest on Great Barrier Island.[4]

Between 1898 and 1908, Mr. Howie delivered thousands of messages. His birds were speedy. They could travel in two hours the distance a boat would traverse in three days. Dependable. Storms rarely knocked the pigeons off course, and they never called in sick. And, most notably, they were accurate. They could find their nest. Why else would we call them homing pigeons?

Other birds fly faster. Other birds are stronger. Other birds boast larger plumes or stronger claws. But none have the navigational skill of the homing pigeon.

Some scientists believe pigeons have traces of magnetite in their beaks and brains that interplay with the magnetic field of the earth.[5] Others credit the birds' sense of hearing. Do they pick up a frequency other birds miss? Or do they sniff out their target with a keen sense of smell?

What we know is this: pigeons have an innate home detector.

So do you.

What God gave pigeons, he gave to you. No, not bird brains. A guidance system. You were born heaven equipped with a hunger for your heavenly home. Need proof?

Consider your questions. Questions about death and time, significance and relevance. Animals don't seem to ask the questions we do. Dogs howl at the moon, but we stare at it. How did we get here? What are we here for? Are we someone's idea or something's accident? Why on earth are we on this earth?

We ask questions about pain. The words *leukemia*

and *child* shouldn't appear in the same sentence. And war. Can't conflict go the way of phonograph records and telegrams? And the grave. Why is the dash between the dates on a tombstone so small? Something tells us this isn't right, good, fair. This isn't home.

From whence come these stirrings? Who put these thoughts in our heads? Why can't we, like rabbits, be happy with carrots and copulation? Because, according to Jesus, we aren't home yet.

Probably his best-known story follows the trail of a homeless runaway. Jesus doesn't give us a name, just a pedigree: rich. Rockefeller rich. Spoiled rich. A silver-spooned, yacht-owning, trust-funded, blue-blooded boy. Rather than learn his father's business, he disregarded his father's kindness, cashed in his stock, and drove his Mercedes to the big city.

As fast as you can say dead broke, he was exactly that. No friends, no funds, no clue what to do. He ended up in a pigpen of trouble. He fed hogs, slept in the mud, and grew so hungry he gave serious consideration to licking the slop. That's when he thought of home. He remembered lasagna and laughter at the dining room table. His warm bed, clean pajamas, and fuzzy slippers. He missed his father's face and longed for his father's voice. He looked around at the snorting pigs and buzzing flies and made a decision.

"I'll turn the pigpen into a home." He took out a loan from the piggy bank and remodeled the place. New throw rug over the mud. A La-Z-Boy recliner next to the trough. He hung a flat screen on the fence post, flipped the slop bucket upside down, and called it a lamp shade. He tied a ribbon on a sow's head and called her honey. He pierced the ear of a piglet and called him son. Within short order he'd made a home out of the pigsty and settled in for the good life.

OK, maybe he didn't. But don't we? Don't we do our best to make this mess a home? Do up and doll up. Revamp and redecorate. We face-lift this. Overhaul that. Salt on the slop and whitewash for the posts. Ribbons for her and tattoos for him. And, in time, the place ain't half bad.

We actually feel at home.

But then the flies come out. People die, earthquakes rumble, and nations rage. Families collapse, and children die of hunger. Dictators snort and treat people like, well, like pigs. And this world stinks.

And we have a choice. We can pretend this life is all God intended. Or . . .

We can come to our senses. We can follow the

example of the prodigal son. "I will set out and go back to my father" (Luke 15:18).

Don't you love the image of the son setting out for the homestead: rising out of the mud, turning his back to the pigs, and turning his eyes toward the father? This is Jesus' invitation to us. Set your hearts on your home. "Seek first the kingdom of God" (Matthew 6:33 NKJV).

In his plan it's all about the King and his kingdom. He wrote the script, built the sets, directs the actors, and knows the final act—an everlasting kingdom. "And this is [God's] plan: At the right time he will bring everything together under the authority of Christ—everything in heaven and on earth" (Ephesians 1:10 NLT).

Reach for it!

The journey home is nice, but the journey is not the goal. I prepared part of this message on an airplane. As I looked around at fellow passengers, I saw content people. Thanks to books, pillows, and crossword puzzles, they passed the time quite nicely. But suppose this announcement were heard: "Ladies and gentlemen, this flight is your final destination. We will never land. Your home is this plane, so enjoy the journey."

Passengers would become mutineers. We'd take over the cockpit and seek a landing strip. We wouldn't settle for such an idea. The journey is not the destination. The vessel is not the goal. Those who are content with nothing more than joy in the journey are settling for too little satisfaction. Our hearts tell us there is more to this life than this life. We, like E.T., lift bent fingers to the sky. We may not know where to point, but we know not to call this airplane our home.

"God ... has planted eternity in the human heart" (Ecclesiastes 3:11 NLT). Mr. Howie released his pigeons from Auckland, and God released his children from the cage of time. Our privilege is to keep flapping until we spot the island. Those who do will discover a spiritual cache, a treasure hidden in a field, a pearl of great value (Matthew 13:44 – 46). Finding the kingdom is like finding a winning lottery ticket in the sock drawer or locating the cover to a jigsaw puzzle box. "Oh, this is how it's going to look."

In God's narrative, life on earth is but the beginning: the first letter of the first sentence in the first chapter of the great story God is writing with your life.

Do you feel as if your best years have passed you by? Hogwash. You will do your best work in heaven. Do you regret wasting seasons of life on foolish pursuits? So do I. But we can stop our laments. We have an eternity to make up for lost time. Are you puzzled by the challenges of your days? Then see yourself as an uncut jewel and God as a lapidary. He is polishing you for your place in his kingdom. Your biggest moments lie ahead, on the other side of the grave.

So "seek those things which are above, where Christ is, sitting at the right hand of God" (Colossians 3:1 NKJV). Scripture uses a starchy verb here. *Zēteite* ("to seek") is to "covet earnestly, strive after, to inquire for, desire, even require."

Seek heaven the way a sailor seeks the coast or a pilot seeks the landing strip or a missile seeks heat. Head for home the way a pigeon wings to the nest or the prodigal strode to his papa. "Think only about" it (3:2 NCV). "Keep your mind" on it (3:2 GWT). "Set your sights on the realities of heaven" (3:1 NLT). "Pursue the things over which Christ presides" (3:1 MSG). Obsess yourself with heaven!

And, for heaven's sake, don't settle for pigpens on earth.

I found myself saying something similar to my nephew and niece. I had taken them to the San Antonio Zoo, a perfect place for a three- and a five-year-old to spend a Saturday afternoon. A veteran kid-guide, I knew the path to take. Start small and end wild. We began with the lowly, glass-caged reptiles. Next we oohed and aahed at the parrots and pink flamingos. We fed the sheep in the petting zoo and tossed crumbs to the fish in the pond. But all along I kept telling Lawson and Callie, "We're getting closer to the big animals. Elephants and tigers are just around the corner."

Finally we reached the Africa section. For full effect I told them to enter with their heads down and their eyes on the sidewalk. I walked them right up to the elephant fence.

And just when I was about to tell them to lift their eyes, Lawson made a discovery. "Look, a doodlebug!"

"Where?" Callie asked.

"Here!" He squatted down and placed the pellet-sized insect in the palm of his hand and began to roll it around.

"Let me see it!" Callie said.

I couldn't lure them away. "Hey, guys, this is the jungle section."

No response.

"Don't you want to see the wild animals?"

No, they focused on the bug. There we stood, elephants to our left, lions to our right, only a stone's throw from hippos and leopards, and what were they doing? Playing with a doodlebug.

Don't we all? Myriads of mighty angels encircle us, the presence of our Maker engulfs us, the witness of a thousand galaxies and constellations calls to us, the flowing tide of God's history carries us, the crowning of Christ as

King of the universe awaits us, but we can't get our eyes off the doodlebugs of life: paychecks, gadgets, vacations, and weekends.

Open your eyes, Christ invites. *Lift up your gaze*. "Seek first the kingdom of God" (Matthew 6:33 NKJV). Limit your world to the doodlebugs of this life, and, mark it down, you will be disappointed. Limit your story to the days between your birth and death, and brace yourself for a sad ending. You were made for more than this life.

Five hundred years ago, sailors feared the horizon. Sail too far and risk falling off the edge, they reasoned. Common wisdom of the ancients warned against the unseen. So did the monument at the Strait of Gibraltar. At its narrowest margin, Spaniards erected a huge marker that bore in its stone the three-word Latin slogan *Ne plus ultra* or "No more beyond."

But then came Christopher Columbus and the voyage of 1492. The discovery of the New World changed everything. Spain acknowledged this in its coins, which came to bear the slogan *plus ultra*—"more beyond."[6]

Why don't you chisel the *no* off your future? God has set your heart on home. Keep flying until you reach it.

CHAPTER FOUR

When You Discover Your Place in God's Plan ...

YOU HEAR A VOICE
YOU CAN TRUST

You think it's hard to walk in the dark? Find it difficult to navigate a room with the lights off or your eyes closed? Try flying a small plane at fifteen thousand feet. Blind.

Jim O'Neill did. Not that he intended to do so. The sixty-five-year-old pilot was forty minutes into a four-hour solo flight from Glasgow, Scotland, to Colchester, England, when his vision failed. He initially thought he had been blinded by the sun but soon realized it was much worse. "Suddenly I couldn't see the dials in front of me. It was just a blur. I was helpless."

He gave new meaning to the phrase "flying blind."

Turns out, he'd suffered a stroke. O'Neill groped and found the radio of his Cessna and issued a Mayday alert.

Paul Gerrard, a Royal Air Force Wing Commander who had just completed a training sortie nearby, was contacted by air traffic controllers and took off in O'Neill's direction. He found the plane and began talking to the stricken pilot.

The commander told O'Neill what to do. His instructions were reassuring and simple: "A gentle right turn, please. Left a bit. Right a bit." He hovered within five hundred feet of O'Neill, shepherding him toward the nearest runway. Upon reaching it, the two began to descend. When asked if he could see the runway below, O'Neill apologized, "No sir, negative." O'Neill would have to land the plane by faith, not by sight. He hit the runway but bounced up again. The same thing happened on the second attempt. But on the eighth try, the blinded pilot managed to make a near-perfect landing.[7]

Can you empathize with O'Neill? Most can. We've been struck, perhaps not with a stroke, but with a divorce, a sick child, or a cancer-ridden body. Not midair, but mid-career, midsemester, midlife. We've lost sight of any safe landing strip and, in desperation, issued our share of Mayday prayers. We know the fear of flying blind.

Unlike O'Neill, however, we hear more than one voice. Many voices besiege our cockpit. The talk show host urges us to worry. The New Age guru says to relax.

The financial page forecasts a downturn. The pastor says pray; the professor says phooey. So many opinions! Lose weight. Eat low fat. Join our church. Try our crystals. It's enough to make you cover your ears and run.

And what if you follow the wrong voice? What if you make the same mistake as the followers of self-help guru James Arthur Ray? He promised to help people achieve spiritual and financial wealth, asserting to "double, triple, even multiply by ten the size of your business."

He gave more than financial counsel to the more than fifty clients who crowded into his 415-square-foot sweat lodge in Sedona, Arizona. They had paid him between nine thousand and ten thousand dollars apiece for a five-day spiritual warrior retreat. The participants had fasted for thirty-six hours as part of a personal spiritual quest, then ate a breakfast buffet before entering the saunalike hut that afternoon. People began passing out and vomiting, but were still urged to stay in the lodge. Two hours later, three of them were dead.[8]

Oh, the voices. How do we select the right one?

A more important question cannot be asked. In fact, a form of the question was asked by Jesus himself: "Who do you say I am?" (Mark 8:29).

He had led his disciples into Caesarea Philippi. The region was to religion what Wal-Mart is to shopping—

every variety in one place. A center of Baal worship. An impressive temple of white marble dedicated to the godhead of Caesar. Shrines to the Syrian gods. Here Jesus, within earshot of every spiritual voice of his era, asked his followers:

> "Who do people say I am?"
>
> They replied, "Some say John the Baptist; others say Elijah; and still others, one of the prophets."
>
> "But what about you?" he asked. "Who do you say I am?"
>
> Peter answered, "You are the Messiah."
>
> MARK 8:27–29

When it came to expressing the opinions of others, the disciples were chatty. Everyone spoke. But when it came to this personal question, only Peter replied. We do well to wonder why. Why only one answer? Was Peter so confident and quick that the others had no time to speak? Did Peter drown out the replies of everyone else?

"YOU ARE THE MESSIAH!"

Maybe Peter's confession echoed off the walls of the temples. Or perhaps it didn't.

Perhaps no one else spoke because no one else knew what to say. Maybe John ducked his eyes. Philip looked away. Andrew cleared his throat. Nathanael kicked the dirt, then elbowed Peter. And Peter sighed. He looked at this lean-faced, homeless teacher from Nazareth and pondered the question, "Who do you say I am?"

It couldn't have been a new one for Peter. He must have asked it a thousand times: the night when Jesus walked off the beach into the bay without sinking, the day he turned a boy's basket into an "all you can eat" buffet, the time he wove a whip and drove the swindlers out of the temple. *Who is this man?*

Peter had asked the question. So have millions of other people. All serious students of Christ, indeed students of life, have stood in their personal version of Caesarea Philippi and contrasted Jesus with the great philosophers of the world and heard him inquire, "Who do you say I am?"

"You're a decent fellow," some have answered. After all, if you can't like Jesus, can you like anyone? In Jesus, the poor found a friend, and the forgotten found an advocate. Jesus was nothing if not good. True-blue. Solid. Dependable. Everyone's first choice for a best friend, right?

Sure, if you want a best friend who claims to be God on earth. For being such an affable sort, Jesus had a curious habit of declaring divinity.

His favorite self-designation was Son of Man. The title

appears eighty-two times in the four gospels, only twice by anyone other than Jesus.[9]

> "The Son of Man has nowhere to lay His head."
> (Matthew 8:20 NKJV)

> "The Son of Man must suffer many things."
> (Mark 8:31 NKJV)

> "They will see the Son of Man coming . . ."
> (Mark 13:26 NKJV)

First-century listeners found the claim outrageous. They were acquainted with its origin in Daniel 7. In his visions the prophet Daniel saw "One like the Son of Man, coming with the clouds of heaven! . . . Then to Him was given dominion and glory and a kingdom, that all peoples, nations, and languages should serve Him. His dominion is an everlasting dominion, which shall not pass away, and His kingdom the one which shall not be destroyed" (Daniel 7:13 – 14 NKJV).

"That's me," Jesus was saying. Every time he used the phrase "Son of Man," he crowned himself. Would a decent fellow walk around making such a claim? You want a guy like this in your neighborhood?

And what about his "I AM" statements? "I am the light

of the world." "I am the bread of life," "the resurrection and the life," and "the way, the truth, and the life." And most stunning, "Before Abraham was born, I am!"[10]

By claiming the "I AM" title, Jesus was equating himself with God.

Jesus claimed to be able to forgive sins — a privilege only God can exercise (Matthew 9:4 – 7). He claimed to be greater than Jonah, Solomon, Jacob, and even Abraham (Matthew 12:38 – 42; John 4:12 – 14; 8:53 – 56). Jesus said that John the Baptist was the greatest man who had ever lived but implied that he was greater (Matthew 11:11). Jesus commanded people to pray in his name (John 14:13 – 14). He claimed to be greater than the temple (Matthew 12:6), greater than the Sabbath (Matthew 12:8). He claimed his words would outlive heaven and earth (Mark 13:31) and that all authority in heaven and on earth had been given to him (Matthew 28:18 – 20).

Does a decent fellow say things like this? No, but a demented fool does.

Maybe Jesus was a megalomaniac on par with Alexander the Great or Adolf Hitler. But, honestly, could a madman do what Jesus did?

Look at the devotion he inspired. People didn't just respect Jesus. They liked him; they left their homes and businesses and followed him. Men and women alike tethered their hope to his life. Impulsive people like Peter. Visionaries like Philip. Passionate men like John, careful men like Thomas, methodical men like Matthew the tax collector. When the men had left Jesus in the grave, it was the women who came to honor him—women from all walks of life, homemaking to philanthropy.

And people were better because of him. Madmen sire madmen: Saddam Hussein created murderers, Joseph Stalin created power addicts, Charles Manson created wackos. But Jesus transformed common dockworkers and net casters into the authors of history's greatest book and founders of its greatest movement. "They stand like a row of noble pillars towering far across the flats of time. But the sunlight that shines on them, and makes them visible, comes entirely from Him. He gave them all their greatness; and theirs is one of the most striking evidences of His."[11]

And what about his teaching? What about the day when Jesus' enemies sent officers to arrest him? Because of the crowd, they couldn't reach him directly. As they were pushing through the people, the officers were so gripped by his words that they abandoned their assignment. Their hearts were arrested, and Jesus was not. They returned to their superiors without a prisoner. Their defense? "No man ever spoke like this Man!" (John 7:46 NKJV).

Christ stunned people with his authority and clarity. His was not the mind of a deranged wild man. Demented fool? No. Deceiving fraud? Some have said so.

Some believe that Jesus masterminded the greatest scheme in the history of humanity, that he out-Ponzied the swindlers and out-hustled the hucksters. If that were true, billions of humans have been fleeced into following a first-century pied piper over the edge of a cliff.

Should we crown Christ as the foremost fraud in the world?

Not too quickly. Look at the miracles Jesus performed. The four gospels detail approximately thirty-six miracles and reference many more. He multiplied bread and fish, changed water into wine, calmed more than one storm, restored sight to more one than blind man. He healed contagious skin diseases, gave steps to the lame, purged demons, stopped a hemorrhage, even replaced a severed ear.

Yet, in doing so, Jesus never grandstanded his miraculous powers. Never went for fame or profit. Jesus performed miracles for two reasons: to prove his identity and to help his people.

Around AD 120, a man named Quadratus wrote the emperor Hadrian, defending Christianity. His apologetic included this sentence: "The works of our Saviour were lasting, for they were genuine: those who were healed and those who were raised from the dead were seen ... not merely while the Saviour was on earth, but also after his death; they were alive for quite a while, so that some of them lived even to our day."[12]

Had Jesus been a fraud or trickster, the Jerusalem congregation would have died a stillborn death. People would have denounced the miracles of Christ. But they did just the opposite. Can you imagine the apostles inviting testimonies? "If you were a part of the crowd he fed, one of the dead he raised, or one of the sick he healed, speak up and tell your story."

And speak they did. The church exploded like a fire on a West Texas prairie. Why? Because Jesus performed public, memorable miracles. He healed people.

And he loved people. He paid no heed to class or nationality, past sins or present accomplishments. The neediest and loneliest found a friend in Jesus:

- a woman scarcely clothed because of last night's affair. Christ befriended and defended her. (John 8:3–11)

- an unscrupulous tax collector left friendless because of his misdealings. Christ became his mentor. (Luke 19:2–10)

    a multiple divorcée who drew from the well
    in the heat of the day to avoid the stares
    of the villagers. Jesus gave her his attention.
    (John 4:5–26)

Could a lying sham love this way? If his intent was to trick people out of their money or worship, he did a pitifully poor job, for he died utterly broke and virtually abandoned.

What if Peter was correct? "You are the Messiah" (Mark 8:29).

What if Jesus really was, and is, the Son of God? If so, then we can relish this wonderful truth: we never travel alone. True, we cannot see the runway. We do not know what the future holds. But, no, we are not alone.

We have what Jim O'Neill had: the commander's voice to guide us home. Let's heed it, shall we? Let's issue the necessary Mayday prayer and follow the guidance that God sends. If so, we will hear what O'Neill heard.

BBC News made the recording of the final four minutes of the flight available. Listen and you'll hear the patient voice of a confident commander. "You've missed the runway this time … Let's start another gentle right-hand turn … Keep the right turn coming … Roll out left … No need to worry … Roll out left. Left again, left again … Keep coming down … Turn left, turn left … Hey, no problem … Can you see the runway now?… So you cannot see the runway?… Keep coming down …"

And then finally, "You are safe to land."[13]

I'm looking forward to hearing that final sentence someday. Aren't you?

CHAPTER FIVE

When You Discover Your Place in God's Plan …

YOU WON'T BE FORSAKEN

TENNESSEE GIVES DRUNK DRIVERS A NEW WARDROBE. THE Volunteer State has a special gift for any person convicted of driving their streets under the influence of alcohol. A blaze orange vest. Offenders are required to wear it in public three different days for eight hours at a time while picking up litter from the side of the highway. Stenciled on the back in four-inch-tall letters are the words "I AM A DRUNK DRIVER."[14]

No doubt they deserve the punishment. In fact, given the threat they've imposed upon the highways, they deserve three days of public humiliation. I don't question the strategy of the state.

But I wonder why we do the same to ourselves. Why we dress ourselves in our mistakes, don the robe of poor choices. Don't we? We step into our closets and sort through our regrets and rebellion and, for some odd reason, vest up.

I DISAPPOINTED MY PARENTS.

I WASTED MY YOUTH.

I NEGLECTED MY KIDS.

Sometimes we cover the vest with a blouse or blazer of good behavior. Mrs. Adams did. She's not the only person who ever came to see me while wearing a vest, but she was the first. I was only days into my first full-time church position in Miami, Florida. I'd barely unpacked my books when the receptionist asked if I could receive a visitor.

The senior minister was occupied, and I was next in line. I stepped into the conference room, where she sat, stirring a cup of coffee. She was a slight woman, wearing a nice dress and carrying a designer purse. She looked at me for only a moment, then back at the cup. That I was several years her junior didn't seem to matter.

"I left my family," she blurted. No greeting, introduction, or small talk. Just a confession.

I took a seat and asked her to tell me about it. I didn't have to ask twice. Too much pressure, temptation, and stress. So she walked out on her kids — ten years before she came to see me! What struck me about her story was not what she had done but how long she'd been living with her guilt. A decade! And now, hungry for help, she had a request.

"Can you give me some work to do?"

"What? Do you need some money?"

She looked at me as though I were a doctor unacquainted with penicillin. "No, I need some work. Anything. Letters to file, floors to sweep. Give me some work to do. I'll feel better if I do some work for God."

Welcome to the vest system. Hard to hide it. Harder still to discard it. But we work at doing so. Emphasis on the word *work*. Overcome bad deeds with good ones. Offset bad choices with godly ones, stupid moves with righteous ones. But the vest-removal process is flawed. No one knows what work to do or how long to do it. Shouldn't the Bible, of all books, tell us? But it doesn't. Instead, the Bible tells us how God's story redeems our story.

Jesus' death on the cross is not a secondary theme in Scripture; it is the core. The English word *crucial* comes from the Latin for cross (*crux*). The crucial accomplishment of Christ occurred on the cross. Lest we miss the message, God encased the climax of his story in high drama.

The garden: Jesus crying out, the disciples running out, the soldiers bursting in.

The trials: early morning mockery and deceit. Jews scoffing. Pilate washing.

The soldiers: weaving thorns, slashing whips, pounding nails.

Jesus: bloodied, beaten. More crimson than clean. Every sinew afire with pain.

And God: He ebonized the sky and shook the earth. He cleaved the rocks and ripped the temple curtain. He untombed the entombed and unveiled the Holy of Holies.

But first he heard the cry of his Son.

"My God, my God, why have you forsaken me?" (Matthew 27:46)

Forsaken. Visceral, painful. The word has the connotations of abandonment, of desertion, of being helpless, alone, cast out, of being completely forgotten.

Jesus forsaken? Does Scripture not declare, "I have not seen the righteous forsaken" and assure that "the Lord . . . does not forsake His saints" (Psalm 37:25, 28 NKJV)?

Indeed it does. But in that hour Jesus was anything but righteous. This was the moment in which "God put the wrong on him who never did anything wrong" (2 Corinthians 5:21 MSG). "God . . . piled all our sins, everything we've done wrong, on him, on him. He was beaten, he was tortured, but he didn't say a word" (Isaiah 53:6–7 MSG).

He dressed Christ in vests. Our vests, each and every one.

I CHEATED MY FRIENDS.

I LIED TO MY WIFE.

I ABUSED MY CHILDREN.

I CURSED MY GOD.

As if Jesus deserved them, he wore them. Our sins, our vests, were put on Christ. "The LORD has laid on him the iniquity of us all" (Isaiah 53:6). "He bore the sin of many" (Isaiah 53:12). Paul proclaimed that God made Christ "to be sin" (2 Corinthians 5:21) and become "a curse for us" (Galatians 3:13). Peter agreed: "'[Jesus] himself bore our sins' in his body on the cross" (1 Peter 2:24).

This is the monumental offer of God. What does God say to the woman who wants to work and offset her guilt? Simple: the work has been done. My Son wore your sin on himself, and I punished it there.

"For Christ also suffered once for sins, the just for the unjust, that He might bring us to God" (1 Peter 3:18 NKJV).

On August 16, 1987, Northwest Airlines flight 255 crashed after taking off from the Detroit airport, killing 155 people. The lone survivor was four-year-old Cecelia from Tempe, Arizona. Rescuers found her in such good condition that they wondered if she'd actually been on the flight. Perhaps she was riding in one of the cars into which the airplane crashed. But, no, her name was on the manifest.

While the exact nature of events may never be known, Cecelia's survival may have been due to her mother's quick response. Initial reports from the scene indicate that, as the plane was falling, her mother, Paula Cichan, unbuckled her own seat belt, got down on her knees in front of her daughter, and wrapped her arms and body around the girl. She separated her from the force of the fall ... and the daughter survived.[15]

God did the same for us. He wrapped himself around us and felt the full force of the fall. He took the unrelaxed punishment of the guilty. He died, not like a sinner, but as a sinner — in our place. "By a wonderful exchange our sins are now not ours but Christ's, and Christ's righteousness is not Christ's but ours."[16] His sacrifice is a sufficient one. Our merits don't enhance it. Our stumbles don't diminish it. The sacrifice of Christ is a total and unceasing and accomplished work.

"It is finished," Jesus announced (John 19:30). His

prayer of abandonment is followed by a cry of accomplishment. Not "It is begun" or "It is initiated" or "It is a work in progress." No, "It is finished."

You can remove your vest. Toss the thing in a trash barrel, and set it on fire. You need never wear it again. Does better news exist? Actually, yes. There is more. We not only remove our vest; we don his! He is "our righteousness" (1 Corinthians 1:30)

God does not simply remove our failures; he dresses us in the goodness of Christ! "For all of you who were baptized into Christ have clothed yourselves with Christ" (Galatians 3:27).

Think about this for a moment. When you make God's story yours, he covers you in Christ. You wear him like a vest. Old labels no longer apply—only labels that would be appropriately worn by Jesus Christ. Can you think of a few phrases for your new vest? How about

- royal priest (1 Peter 2:9)

- complete (Colossians 2:10 NKJV)

- free from condemnation (Romans 8:1)

- secure (John 10:28)

- established and anointed one
  (2 Corinthians 1:21 NKJV)

- God's coworker (2 Corinthians 6:1)

- God's temple (1 Corinthians 3:16–17)

- God's workmanship (Ephesians 2:10 NKJV)

How do you like that outfit?

"Now you're dressed in a new wardrobe. Every item of your new way of life is custom-made by the Creator, with his label on it. All the old fashions are now obsolete" (Colossians 3:10 MSG). Don't mess with the old clothes any longer. "As far as the east is from the west, so far has he removed our transgressions from us" (Psalm 103:12). How far is the east from the west? Further and further by the moment. Travel west and you can make laps around the globe and never go east. Journey east and, if you desire, maintain an easterly course indefinitely. Not so with the other two directions. If you go north or south, you'll eventually reach the North or South Pole and change directions. But east and west have no turning points.

Neither does God. When he sends your sins to the east and you to the west, you can be sure of this: he doesn't see you in your sins. His forgiveness is irreversible. "He does not treat us as our sins deserve or repay us according to our iniquities" (Psalm 103:10).

Headline this truth: when God sees you, he sees his

Son, not your sin. God "blots out your transgressions" and "remembers your sins no more" (Isaiah 43:25). No probation. No exception. No reversals.

He did his due diligence. He saw your secret deeds and heard your unsaid thoughts. The lies, the lusts, the longings—he knows them all. God assessed your life from first day to last, from worst moment to best, and made his decision.

"I want that child in my kingdom."

You cannot convince him otherwise.

Look on his city gates for proof. In the last pages of the Bible, John describes the entrance to the New Jerusalem:

> She had a great and high wall with twelve gates ... and names written on them, which are the names of the twelve tribes of the children of Israel....
>
> Now the wall of the city had twelve foundations, and on them were the names of the twelve apostles of the Lamb.
>
> REVELATION 21:12, 14 NKJV

God engraved the names of the sons of Jacob on his gateposts. More ragamuffins than reverends. Their rap sheets include stories of mass murder (Genesis 34), incest (38:13–18), and brotherly betrayal (37:17–28). They behaved more like the 3:00 a.m. nightclub crowd than a Valhalla of faith. Yet God carved their names on the New Jerusalem gates.

And dare we mention the names on the foundations? Peter, the apostle who saved his own skin instead of his Savior's. James and John, who jockeyed for VIP seats in heaven. Thomas, the dubious, who insisted on a personal audience with the resurrected Jesus. These were the disciples who told the children to leave Jesus alone (Luke 18:15), who told Jesus to leave the hungry on their own (Matthew 14:15), and chose to leave Jesus alone to face his crucifixion (Matthew 26:36–45). Yet all their names appear on the foundations. Matthew's does. Peter's does. Bartholomew's does.

And yours? It's not engraved in the gate, but it is written in the Book of the Lamb. Not in pencil marks that can be erased, but with blood that will not be removed. No need to keep God happy; he is satisfied. No need to pay the price; Jesus paid it.

All.

Lose your old vest. You look better wearing his.

CHAPTER SIX

When You Discover Your Place in God's Plan ...

YOUR FINAL CHAPTER BECOMES A PREFACE

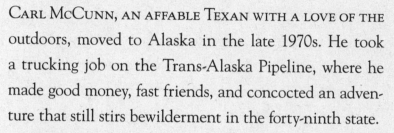

CARL MCCUNN, AN AFFABLE TEXAN WITH A LOVE OF THE outdoors, moved to Alaska in the late 1970s. He took a trucking job on the Trans-Alaska Pipeline, where he made good money, fast friends, and concocted an adventure that still stirs bewilderment in the forty-ninth state.

At the age of thirty-five, he embarked on a five-month photography expedition in the wild. Friends describe how seriously he prepared for the quest, devoting a year to plan making and detail checking. He solicited advice and purchased supplies. And then, in March 1981, he hired a bush pilot to drop him at a remote lake near the Coleen River, some seventy miles northeast of Fort Yukon. He took two rifles, a shotgun, fourteen hundred pounds of provisions, and five hundred rolls of film.

He set up his tent and set about his season of isolation, blissfully unaware of an overlooked detail that would cost him his life.

He had made no arrangement to be picked up.

His unbelievable blunder didn't dawn on him until August. We know this because of a hundred-page loose-leaf diary the Alaska state troopers found near his body the following February. In an understatement the size of Mount McKinley, McCunn wrote: "I think I should have used more foresight about arranging my departure."

As the days shortened and air chilled, he began searching the ground for food and the skies for rescue. He was running low on ammunition. Hiking out was impossible. He had no solution but to hope someone in the city would notice his absence.

By the end of September, the snow was piling, the lake was frozen, and supplies were nearly gone. His body fat began to metabolize, making it more difficult to stay warm. Temperatures hovered around zero, and frostbite began to attack his fingers and toes. ·

By late November, McCunn was out of food, strength, and optimism. One of his final diary entries reads, "This is sure a slow and agonizing way to die."[17]

Isolated with no rescue. Trapped with no exit. Nothing to do but wait for the end. Chilling.

And puzzling. Why no exit strategy? Didn't he know that every trip comes to an end? It's not like his excursion would last forever.

Ours won't.

This heart will feel a final pulse. These lungs will empty a final breath. The hand that directs this pen across the page will fall limp and still. Barring the return of Christ, I will die. So will you. "Death is the most democratic institution on earth. . . . It allows no discrimination, tolerates no exceptions. The mortality rate of mankind is the same the world over: one death per person."[18]

Or, as the psalmist asked, "Who can live and not see death, or who can escape the power of the grave?" (Psalm 89:48). Young and old, good and bad, rich and poor. Neither gender is spared; no class is exempt. "No one has power over the time of their death" (Ecclesiastes 8:8).

The geniuses, the rich, the poor — no one outruns it or outsmarts it. Julius Caesar died. Elvis died. John Kennedy died. Princess Diana died. We all die. Nearly 2 people a second, more than 6,000 an hour, more than 155,000 every day, about 57 million a year.[19] We don't escape death.

The finest surgeon might enhance your life but can't eliminate your death. The Hebrew writer was blunt: "People are destined to die once" (Hebrews 9:27). Exercise all you want. Eat nothing but health food, and pop fistfuls of vitamins. Stay out of the sun, away from alcohol, and off drugs. Do your best to stay alive, and, still, you die.

Death seems like such a dead end.

Until we read Jesus' resurrection story.

"He is not here. He has risen from the dead as he said he would" (Matthew 28:6 NCV).

It was Sunday morning after the Friday execution. Jesus' final breath had sucked the air out of the universe. As his body seemed to be a-moldering in the grave, no one was placing bets on a resurrection.

His enemies were satisfied with their work. The spear to his side guaranteed his demise. His tongue was silenced. His last deed done. They raised a toast to a dead Jesus. Their only concern was those pesky disciples. The religious leaders made this request of Pilate: "So give the order for the tomb to be made secure until the third day. Otherwise, his disciples may come and steal the body and tell the people that he has been raised from the dead" (Matthew 27:64).

No concern was necessary. The disciples were at melt-down. When Jesus was arrested, "all the disciples forsook Him and fled" (Matthew 26:56 NKJV). Peter followed from a distance but caved in and cursed Christ. John watched Jesus die, but we have no record that John gave any thought to ever seeing him again. The other followers didn't even linger; they cowered in Jerusalem's cupboards and corners for fear of the cross that bore their names.

No one dreamed of a Sunday morning miracle. Peter didn't ask John, "What will you say when you see Jesus?" Mary didn't ponder, *How will he appear?* They didn't encourage each other with quotes of his promised return. They could have. At least four times Jesus had said words like these: "The Son of Man is being betrayed into the hands of men, and they will kill Him. And after He is killed, He will rise the third day."[20] You'd think someone would mention this prophecy and do the math. "Hmm, he died yesterday. Today is the second day. He promised to rise on the third day. Tomorrow is the third day … Friends, I think we'd better wake up early tomorrow."

But Saturday saw no such plans. On Saturday the Enemy had won, courage was gone, and hope caught the last train to the coast. They planned to embalm Jesus, not talk to him.

When the Sabbath was over, Mary Magdalene, Mary the mother of James, and Salome bought spices so that they might go to anoint Jesus' body. Very early on the first day of the week, just after sunrise, they were on their way to the tomb and they asked each other, "Who will roll the stone away from the entrance of the tomb?"

MARK 16:1–3

Easter parade? Victory march? Hardly. More like a funeral procession. It may have been Sunday morning, but their world was stuck on Saturday.

It was left to the angel to lead them into Sunday.

There was a violent earthquake, for an angel of the Lord came down from heaven and, going to the tomb, rolled back the stone and sat on it. His appearance was like lightning, and his clothes were white as snow. The guards were so afraid of him that they shook and became like dead men.

The angel said to the women, "Do not be afraid, for I know that you are looking for Jesus, who was crucified. He is not here; he has risen, just as he said. Come and see the place where he lay."

MATTHEW 28:2–6

God shook up the cemetery. Trees swayed, and the ground trembled. Pebbles bounced, and the women struggled to maintain their balance. They looked in the direction of the tomb only to see the guards—scared stiff, paralyzed, and sprawled on the ground. Hard to miss the irony: the guards of the dead appear dead, while the dead one appears to be living. Take that, Devil. Remember the famous play on Nietzsche's statement?[21]

"GOD is DEAD!"

Nietzsche.

"NIETZSCHE is DEAD!"

God.

The angel sat on the dislodged tombstone. He did not stand in defiance or crouch in alertness. He sat. Legs crossed and whistling? In my imagination at least. The angel sat upon the *stone*. Again, the irony. The very rock intended to mark the resting place of a dead Christ became the resting place of his living angel. And then the announcement.

"He has risen."

Three words in English. Just one in Greek. *Ēgerthē*. So much rests on the validity of this one word. If it is false, then the whole of Christianity collapses like a poorly told joke. Yet, if it is true, then God's story has turned your final chapter into a preface. If the angel was correct, then you can believe this: Jesus descended into the coldest cell of death's prison and allowed the warden to lock the door and smelt the keys in a furnace. And just when the demons began to dance and prance, Jesus pressed pierced hands against the inner walls of the cavern. From deep within he shook the cemetery. The ground rumbled, and the tombstones tumbled.

And out he marched, the cadaver turned king, with the mask of death in one hand and the keys of heaven in the other. *Ēgerthē!* He has risen!

Not risen from sleep. Not risen from confusion. Not risen from stupor or slumber. Not spiritually raised from the dead; *physically* raised. The women and disciples didn't see a phantom or experience a sentiment. They saw Jesus in the flesh. "It is I myself!" he assured them (Luke 24:39).

The Emmaus-bound disciples thought Jesus was a fellow pilgrim. His feet touched the ground. His hands touched the bread. Mary mistook him for a gardener. Thomas studied his wounds. The disciples ate fish that he cooked. The resurrected Christ did physical deeds in a physical body. "I am not a ghost," he explained (Luke 24:39 NLT). "Handle Me and see, for a spirit does not have flesh and bones as you see I have" (verse 39 NKJV).

The bodily resurrection means everything. If Jesus lives on only in spirit and deeds, he is but one of a thousand dead heroes. But if he lives on in flesh and bone, he is the King who pressed his heel against the head of death. What he did with his own grave he promises to do with yours: empty it.

A curious thing happened as I was rewriting this chapter. While reading the above paragraph, I heard my computer signal an e-mail arrival. I stopped to read it. A friend had just returned from the funeral of his ninety-six-year-old aunt, and he wanted to tell me about it.

Max,

Until about a year ago, you couldn't keep up with my Aunt Wanda. Seriously—she had such energy you just couldn't believe it. Her eyesight was failing so completely that her energy almost made it dangerous to go to unfamiliar places with her. Her eyes couldn't see the crack in the sidewalk that she was about to trot over at ninety miles an hour!!!

About a year ago she started having difficulty breathing. The doctor found a mass in her chest that was almost certainly cancer. But at ninety-five there was little reason to do surgery—even exploratory. The better plan was to keep her comfortable.

It was only in the last three days of her life that the mass became painful to the point she needed medication to fight the pain. It became so severe so quickly that she was given enough morphine to sedate her and basically keep her in an unconscious state.

But as she began to pass from this world into the

next, her sight became clear, she was released of the
pain, and even in her unconscious state, she began to
have conversations with those who had gone before
her. She saw her mother (who was her best friend) and
talked to her. And, my favorite part, she saw my dad
and their brother.

My dad and their brother (Uncle Marvin) were
constantly playing practical jokes on their sister (Aunt
Wanda). She always referred to them as "the boys" or
"those boys." I have no idea what they did or how they
greeted her at heaven's door, but whatever it was made
her laugh so hard that she literally pulled her legs up to
her chest and doubled over laughing. "I can't believe you
boys! Oh, my goodness . . . you boys!" She literally took
her last breaths laughing. I can't wait to find out what
she saw. But she saw something grand!"[22]

You will too.

Will you die laughing? I don't know. But die in peace,
for certain. Death is not the final chapter in your story. In
death you will step into the arms of the One who declared,
"I am the resurrection and the life. The one who believes
in me will live, even though they die; and whoever lives
by believing in me will never die" (John 11:25–26).

Winston Churchill believed this. The prime minister

planned his own funeral. According to his instructions, two buglers were positioned high in the dome of St. Paul's Cathedral. At the conclusion of the service, the first one played taps, the signal of a day completed. Immediately thereafter, with the sounds of the first song still ringing in the air, the second bugler played reveille, the song of a day begun.[23]

Appropriate song. Death is no pit but a passageway, not a crisis but a corner turn. Dominion of the grim reaper? No. Territory of the Soul Keeper, who will some-day announce, "Your dead will live, your corpses will get to their feet. All you dead and buried, wake up! Sing! Your dew is morning dew catching the first rays of sun, the earth bursting with life, giving birth to the dead" (Isaiah 26:19 MSG).

Play on, bugler. Play on.

CHAPTER SEVEN

When You Discover Your Place in God's Plan ...

POWER MOVES IN

WHAT GOT INTO PETER? SEVEN WEEKS AGO HE WAS HID-
ing because of Jesus; today he is proclaiming the death
of Jesus. Before the crucifixion, he denied Christ; now
he announces Christ. On the eve of Good Friday, you
couldn't get him to speak up. Today, you can't get him to
shut up! "My fellow Jews, and all of you who are in Jerusalem, listen to me. Pay attention to what I have to say"
(Acts 2:14 NCV).

What got into Peter?

He was a coward at the crucifixion. A kind coward
but a coward nonetheless. A comment from a servant girl
undid him. A soldier didn't bludgeon him. The Sanhedrin
didn't browbeat him. Rome didn't threaten to export him
to Siberia. No, a waitress from the downtown diner heard

his accent and said he knew Jesus. Peter panicked. He not only denied his Lord; he bleeped the very idea. "Then Peter began to place a curse on himself and swear, 'I don't know the man!'" (Matthew 26:74 NCV).

But look at him on the day of Pentecost, declaring to a throng of thousands, "God has made Jesus—the man you nailed to the cross—both Lord and Christ" (Acts 2:36 NCV). Gutsy language. Lynch mobs feed on these accusations. The same crowd that shouted, "Crucify him!" could crucify him.

From wimp to warrior in fifty days. What happened?

Oh, how we need to know. We admire the Pentecost Peter yet identify with the Passover one. We battle addictions we can't shake, pasts we can't escape, bills we can't pay, sorrow that won't fade.

Our convictions wrinkle, and resolve melts. And we wonder why. We look at other believers and ask, Why is her life so fruitful and mine so barren? Why is his life so powerful and mine so weak? Aren't we saved by the same Christ? Don't we read the same Scripture and rally around the same cross? Why do some look like the early Peter and others like the latter? Or, better question, why do I vacillate between the two in any given week?

Jesus embedded an answer in his final earthly message. He told Peter and the other followers, "Wait here to receive the promise from the Father which I told you about. John baptized people with water, but in a few days you will be baptized with the Holy Spirit" (Acts 1:4–5 NCV).

What got into Peter?

God's Spirit did. Ten days after Jesus' ascension into heaven, "all of them were filled with the Holy Spirit" (Acts 2:4). The followers experienced a gushing forth, a tremendous profusion. They were drenched in power. They all were "sons and daughters ... young men ... old men ... servants, both men and women" (Acts 2:17–18). The Holy Spirit, in his own time and according to his own way, filled the followers with supernatural strength.

Didn't Jesus promise this event? As his days on earth came to an end, he said, "But very truly I tell you, it is for your good that I am going away. Unless I go away, the Advocate will not come to you; but if I go, I will send him to you" (John 16:7).

The bad news: Jesus was going away. The wonderful news: Jesus was sending them the Spirit. During his earthly ministry Jesus lived near the disciples. The Holy Spirit, however, would live *in* the disciples. What Jesus did with the followers, the Spirit would do through them and us. Jesus healed; the Spirit heals through us. Jesus taught; the Spirit teaches through us. Jesus comforted; the Spirit comforts through us. The Spirit continues the work of Christ.

The Holy Spirit is not enthusiasm, compassion, or bravado. He might stimulate such emotions, but he himself is a person. He determines itineraries (Acts 16:6), distributes spiritual gifts (1 Corinthians 12:7–11), and selects church leaders (Acts 13:2). He teaches (John 14:26), guides (John 16:13), and comforts (John 16:7 KJV).

"He dwells with you and will be in you" (John 14:17 NKJV). Occasional guest? No sir. The Holy Spirit is a year-round resident in the hearts of his children. As God's story becomes our story, his power becomes our power. Then why do we suffer from power failures?

I believe we make the mistake the Welsh woman made. She lived many years ago in a remote valley but determined that it would be worth the cost and trouble to have electricity in her home. Several weeks after the installation, the power company noticed that she had barely used any. So they sent a meter reader to see what was wrong.

"Is there a problem?" he asked.

"No," she answered, "we're quite satisfied. Every night we turn on the electric lights to see how to light our lamps."[24]

We're prone to do likewise: depend on God's Spirit

to save us but not sustain us. We are like the Galatians whom Paul asked, "After beginning by means of the Spirit, are you now trying to finish by means of the flesh?" (Galatians 3:3). We turn to him to get us started, and then continue in our own strength.

The Christians in Ephesus did this. The apostle Paul assured them that they had received the Spirit. God "put his special mark of ownership on you by giving you the Holy Spirit that he had promised" (Ephesians 1:13 NCV). Even so, he had to urge them to be "filled with the Spirit" (Ephesians 5:18). Interesting. Can a person be saved and not full of the Holy Spirit? They were in Ephesus.

And in Jerusalem. When the apostles instructed the church to select deacons, they said, "So, brothers and sisters, choose seven of your own men who are good, full of the Spirit and full of wisdom" (Acts 6:3 NCV). The fact that men "full of the Spirit" were to be chosen suggests that men lacking in the Spirit were present. We can have the Spirit but not let the Spirit of God have us.

When God's Spirit directs us, we actually "keep in step with the Spirit" (Galatians 5:25). He is the drum major; we are the marching band. He is the sergeant; we are the platoon. He directs and leads; we obey and follow. Not always that easy, is it? We tend to go our own way.

Some time ago I purchased a new cartridge for my

computer printer. But when I used it, no letters appeared on the page. It was half an hour before I noticed the thin strip of tape covering the outlet of the cartridge. There was plenty of ink, but until the tape was removed, no impression could be made.

Is there anything in your life that needs to be removed? Any impediment to the impression of God's Spirit? We can grieve the Spirit with our angry words (Ephesians 4:29–30; Isaiah 63:10) and resist the Spirit in our disobedience (Acts 7:51). We can test or conspire against the Spirit in our plottings (Acts 5:9). We can even quench the Spirit by having no regard for God's teachings. "Never damp the fire of the Spirit, and never despise what is spoken in the name of the Lord" (1 Thessalonians 5:19–20 Phillips).

Here is something that helps me stay in step with the Spirit. We know that the "fruit of the Spirit is love, joy, peace, patience, kindness, goodness, faithfulness, gentleness, self-control" (Galatians 5:22–23 nasb). God's Spirit creates and distributes these characteristics. They are indicators on my spiritual dashboard. So whenever I sense them, I know I am walking in the Spirit. Whenever I lack them, I know I am out of step with the Spirit.

I sensed his corrective pull just yesterday at a Sunday service. A dear woman stopped me as I was entering the building. She didn't agree with a comment I had made in a sermon the week before and wanted to express her opinion … in the foyer … in a loud voice … ten minutes prior to the service.

What's more, she pressed the nerve of my pet peeve. "Other people feel the same way." Grrr. Who are these "other people"? How many "other people" are there? And why, for crying out loud, don't "other people" come and talk to me?

By now it was time for the service to begin. I was more in a mood to hunt bear than to preach. I couldn't get my mind off the woman and the "other people." I drove home from the morning assembly beneath a cloud. Rather than love, joy, peace, and patience, I felt anger, frustration, and impatience. I was completely out of step with the Spirit. And I had a choice. I could march to my own beat, or I could get back in rhythm. I knew what to do.

I made the phone call. "I didn't feel like we quite finished the conversation we began in the foyer," I told her. So we did. And over the next fifteen minutes, we discovered that our differences were based on a misunderstanding, and I learned that the "other people" consisted of her and her husband, and he was really OK.

To walk in the Spirit, respond to the promptings God gives you.

Don't sense any nudging? Just be patient and wait. Jesus told the disciples to "*wait* for the gift my Father promised … the Holy Spirit" (Acts 1:4–5, emphasis mine). Abraham waited for the promised son. Moses waited forty years in the wilderness. Jesus waited thirty years before he began his ministry. God instills seasons of silence in his plan. Winter is needed for the soil to bear fruit. Time is needed for the development of a crop. And disciples wait for the move of God. Wait for him to move, nudge, and direct you. Somewhat as I'm learning to wait on my dance teacher.

Yes, Denalyn and I are taking dance lessons. This was her announcement to me on our twenty-eighth wedding anniversary. She's been making such comments for years. "We need to learn to dance, honey." "What's there to learn?" was my stock reply, and I would remind her of the night we waltzed our way across the dance floor at my niece's wedding reception in 1985. She would mumble something about tractor-trailers having more finesse and drop the subject.

Of late she's been picking it back up. Now that our third little bird has winged her way out of our nest, it's time for the Mr. and Mrs. to slide their heels. So for my anniversary gift, she loaded me in the car, drove me to a shopping center, and parked in front of the Fred Astaire Dance Studio. (I know where they got the name. I just sat there and … uh … stared.)

Our instructor is young enough to be our son. He wears a moustache-less beard and an innocent smile, and I wonder if he'd more quickly teach an elephant to pirouette than me to waltz. He spent the better part of the first class reminding me to "gently lead" my wife. "Place your hand beneath her shoulder blade and guide her."

He said I shoved and dragged her. Denalyn agreed. And to convey his point, he danced with me. He matched one hand on mine, placed the other beneath my left shoulder blade, and off we went, *forward, forward, slide, slide*, following the beat of Barry Manilow across the room. I know, it's not a pretty sight. But it was a good lesson. I learned to follow his lead. He nudged me this way, led me that way, and at the end I even did a nice twirl.

(Just kidding about the twirl. It was more of a tumble.)

It's nice to be led by a master. Won't you let your Master lead you?

> He guides the humble in what is right
> and teaches them his way.
>
> PSALM 25:9

Whether you turn to the right or to the left, your
ears will hear a voice behind you, saying, "This is
the way; walk in it."

ISAIAH 30:21

Wait on the Spirit. If Peter and the apostles needed
his help, don't we? They walked with Jesus for three years,
heard his preaching, and saw his miracles. They saw the
body of Christ buried in the grave and raised from the
dead. They witnessed his upper room appearance and
heard his instruction. Had they not received the best possible training? Weren't they ready?

Yet Jesus told them to wait on the Spirit. "Do not
leave Jerusalem, but wait for the gift my Father promised
… the Holy Spirit" (Acts 1:4–5).

Learn to wait, to be silent, to listen for his voice. Cherish stillness; sensitize yourself to his touch. "Just think—
you don't need a thing, you've got it all! All God's gifts are
right in front of you as you *wait expectantly* for our Master
Jesus to arrive on the scene" (1 Corinthians 1:7–8 MSG,
emphasis mine). You needn't hurry or scurry. The Spirit-
led life does not panic; it trusts.

God's power is very great for us who believe. That
power is the same as the great strength God used to

114

raise Christ from the dead and put him at his right
side in the heavenly world.

EPHESIANS 1:19–20 NCV

The same hand that pushed the rock from the tomb
can shove away your doubt. The same power that stirred
the still heart of Christ can stir your flagging faith. The
same strength that put Satan on his heels can, and will,
defeat Satan in your life. Just keep the power supply open.
Who knows, you may soon hear people asking, "What's
gotten into you?"

CHAPTER EIGHT

When You Discover Your Place in God's Plan ...

THE RIGHT
DOORS OPEN

I CAME HOME THE OTHER DAY TO A HOUSE OF BLOCKED doors. Not just shut doors, closed doors, or locked doors. Blocked doors.

Blame them on Molly, our nine-year-old, ninety-pound golden retriever, who, on most fronts, is a great dog. When it comes to kids and company, Molly sets a tail-wagging standard. But when it comes to doors, Molly just doesn't get it. Other dogs bark when they want out of the house; Molly scratches the door. She is the canine version of Freddy Krueger. Thanks to her, each of our doors has Molly marks.

We tried to teach her to bark, whine, or whistle; no luck. Molly thinks doors are meant to be clawed. So Dena-lyn came up with a solution: doggy doors. She installed

Molly-sized openings on two of our doors, and to teach Molly to use them, Denalyn blocked every other exit. She stacked furniture five feet deep and twice as wide. Molly got the message. She wasn't going out those doors.

And her feelings were hurt. I came home to find her with drooping ears and limp tail. She looked at the blocked door, then at us. "How could you do this to me?" her eyes pleaded. She walked from stack to stack. She didn't understand what was going on.

Maybe you don't either. You try one door after another, yet no one responds to your résumé. No university accepts your application. No doctor has a solution for your illness. No buyers look at your house.

Obstacles pack your path. Road, barricaded. Doorway, padlocked. You, like Molly, walk from one blocked door to another. Do you know the frustration of a blocked door? If so, you have a friend in the apostle Paul.

He, Silas, and Timothy were on their second missionary journey. On his first one Paul enjoyed success at every stop. "They began to report all things that God had done with them and how He had opened a door of faith to the Gentiles" (Acts 14:27 NASB). God opened doors into Cyprus, Antioch, and Iconium. He opened the door of grace at the Jerusalem council and spurred spiritual growth in every city. "The churches were being strength-

ened in the faith, and were increasing in number daily"
(Acts 16:5 NASB).

The missionaries felt the gusts at their backs, and
then, all of a sudden, headwinds.

> Paul and his companions traveled throughout the
> region of Phrygia and Galatia, having been kept
> by the Holy Spirit from preaching the word in the
> province of Asia. When they came to the border of
> Mysia, they tried to enter Bithynia, but the Spirit of
> Jesus would not allow them to.
>
> ACTS 16:6–7

Paul set his sights on Asia. Yet no doors opened. So
the three turned north into Bithynia but encountered
more blocked doors. They jiggled the knobs and pressed
against the entrances but no access. We aren't told how or
why God blocked the door. Just that he did.

He still does.

God owns the key to every door. He is "opening doors
no one can lock, locking doors no one can open" (Revelation 3:7 MSG). Once God closes a door, no one can open
it. Once God shut the door of Noah's ark, only he could
open it. Once he directed the soldiers to seal the tomb of
Jesus, only he could open it. Once he blocks a door, we

cannot open it. During a season of blocked doors, we, like Molly, can grow frustrated.

A few years ago, many of us at Oak Hills were convinced that our church needed a new sanctuary. We were bursting at the seams. Wouldn't God want us to build a larger auditorium? We thought so. We prayed for forty days and sought counsel from other churches. We weighed our options and designed a new facility. Sensing no divine reservation, we began the campaign.

All of a sudden the wind turned. In less than six months, construction costs increased 70 percent! Gulp. Still, we continued. We reduced the scope of the project and challenged the congregation to ante up more money. Even with their astounding generosity, we didn't raise enough money to build the sanctuary. I will never forget the weight I felt when I announced our decision not to build.

Didn't we pray? Didn't we seek God's will? Why would God close the door? Might it have something to do with this—the worst recession since the Great Depression looming less than a year away? God was protecting us. Moreover, within three months I would be diagnosed with a heart condition. God was protecting us.

It was a classic God's story/our story contrast. From our perspective we saw setbacks. God, however, saw an opportunity, an opportunity to keep us out of dangerous debt and bolster our leadership team with a new senior minister, Randy Frazee. A plan to protect us from a budget-busting mortgage and to grant us fresh leadership. God closed the wrong doors so he could lead us through the right one.

As you discover your place in God's story, closed doors take on a new meaning. You no longer see them as interruptions of your plan but as indications of God's plan.

This is what Paul learned. God blocked his missionary team from going north, south, or east. Only west remained, so they ended up at Asia's westernmost point. They stood with their toes in the sand and looked out over the sea. As they slept, "Paul had a vision of a man of Macedonia standing and begging him, 'Come over to Macedonia and help us'" (Acts 16:9).

The closed doors in Asia led to an open-armed invitation to Europe. "Therefore, sailing from Troas, we ran a straight course to Samothrace, and the next day came to Neapolis, and from there to Philippi" (Acts 16:11–12 NKJV). They ran a "straight course." The wind was at their back. Blocked passages became full sails.

After several days Paul and his team went out of the city of Philippi to the riverside to attend a Jewish prayer service. While there, they met Lydia. "One of those listening was a woman from the city of Thyatira named Lydia, a dealer in purple cloth. She was a worshiper of God. The Lord opened her heart to respond to Paul's message" (Acts 16:14).

Read that verse too quickly, and you'll miss this account of the first convert in the West. Christianity was born in the East, and here the seeds of grace rode the winds of sovereignty over the Aegean Sea, fell on Grecian soil, and bore fruit in Philippi. Christ had his first European disciple ... and she was a she!

Is Lydia the reason the Holy Spirit blocked Paul's path? Was God ready to highlight the value of his daughters? Perhaps. In a culture that enslaved and degraded women, God elevated them to salvation co-heirs with men. Proof? The first person in the Western world to receive the Christian promise or host a Christian missionary was a female.

With her support Paul and his team got to work. Their efforts in Philippi were so effective that the pagan religious leaders were angered. They saw the people turning away from the temples and feared the loss of income. So they conjured up a story against Paul and Silas.

Then the multitude rose up together against them; and the magistrates tore off their clothes and commanded them to be beaten with rods. And when they had laid many stripes on them, they threw them into prison, commanding the jailer to keep them securely. Having received such a charge, he put them into the inner prison and fastened their feet in the stocks.

ACTS 16:22–24 NKJV

Listen closely. Do you hear it? The old, familiar sound of keys turning and locks clicking. This time the doors swung closed on the hinges of a prison. Paul and Silas could have groaned, "Oh no, not again. Not another locked door."

But they didn't complain. From the bowels of the prison emerged the most unexpected of sounds: praise and prayer. "About midnight Paul and Silas were praying and singing hymns to God, and the other prisoners were listening to them" (Acts 16:25).

Their feet were in stocks, yet their minds were in heaven. How could they sing at a time like this? The doors were slammed shut. Their feet were clamped. Backs ribboned with wounds. From whence came their song? There is only one answer: they trusted God and aligned their story to his.

The ways of the LORD are right;
the righteous walk in them.

HOSEA 14:9

"God will always give what is right to his people
who cry to him night and day, and he will not be
slow to answer them."

LUKE 18:7 NCV

When God locks a door, it needs to be locked. When
he blocks a path, it needs to be blocked. When he stuck
Paul and Silas in prison, God had a plan for the prison
jailer. As Paul and Silas sang, God shook the prison. "At
once all the prison doors flew open, and everyone's chains
came loose" (Acts 16:26).

There God goes again, blasting open the most secure
doors in town. When the jailer realized what had happened, he assumed all the prisoners had escaped. He drew
his sword to take his life.

When Paul told him otherwise, the jailer brought the
two missionaries out and asked, "What must I do to be
saved?" (Acts 16:30). Paul told him to believe. He did, and
he and all his family were baptized. The jailer washed their
wounds, and Jesus washed his sins. God shut the door of
the jail cell so that he could open the heart of the jailer.

God uses closed doors to advance his cause.

He closed the womb of a young Sarah so he could display his power to the elderly one.

He shut the palace door on Moses the prince so he could open shackles through Moses the liberator.

He marched Daniel out of Jerusalem so he could use Daniel in Babylon.

And Jesus. Yes, even Jesus knew the challenge of a blocked door. When he requested a path that bypassed the cross, God said no. He said no to Jesus in the garden of Gethsemane so he could say yes to us at the gates of heaven.

God's goal is people. He'll stir up a storm to display his power. He'll keep you out of Asia so you'll speak to Lydia. He'll place you in prison so you'll talk to the jailer. He might even sideline a quarterback in the biggest game of the season. This happened in the 2010 BCS National Championship Game. Colt McCoy, the University of Texas quarterback, had enjoyed four years of open doors. He was the winningest signal caller in the history of collegiate football. But in the National Championship Game, the most important contest of his university career, a shoulder injury put him out of the game in the first quarter. "Slam" went the door. Colt spent most of the game in the locker room.

I don't know if he, like Paul and Silas, was singing, but we know he was trusting. For after the game, he said these words:

> I love this game.... I've done everything I can to contribute to my team.... It's unfortunate I didn't get to play. I would have given everything I had to be out there with my team. But ... I always give God the glory. I never question why things happen the way they do. God is in control of my life. And I know that, if nothing else, I'm standing on the rock.[25]

Even on a bad night, Colt gave testimony to a good God. Did God close the door on the game so he could open the door of a heart?

Colt's father would say so. A young football player approached Brad McCoy after he returned from the game and asked, "I heard what your son said after the game, but I have one question. What is the rock?" McCoy responded, "Well, son, we sing about him at church," and began singing the hymn:

> *My hope is built on nothing less*
> *Than Jesus' blood and righteousness.*
> *I dare not trust the sweetest frame,*

But wholly lean on Jesus' Name.
On Christ, the solid Rock, I stand,
All other ground is sinking sand;
All other ground is sinking sand.[26]

It's not that our plans are bad but that God's plans are better.

"My thoughts are nothing like your thoughts,"
    says the LORD.
  "And my ways are far beyond anything you
      could imagine.
For just as the heavens are higher than
      the earth,
  so my ways are higher than your ways
  and my thoughts higher than your thoughts."

ISAIAH 55:8–9 NLT

This is what I'm trying to teach Molly. Our family blocks doors so she can have better doors.

And this is what God is trying to teach us. Your blocked door doesn't mean God doesn't love you. Quite the opposite. It's proof that he does.

CHAPTER NINE

When You Discover Your Place in God's Plan ...

ALL THINGS WORK FOR GOOD

Robben Island consists of three square miles of windswept land off the southern tip of Africa. Over the centuries it has served as the home for a prison, leper colony, mental asylum, and naval base. Most significantly, it was the home of one of the most famous political prisoners in history, Nelson Mandela.

He opposed the South African apartheid, a system designed to extend the rule and privileges of the white minority and diminish those of the blacks. It ensured that the 14 percent minority would control the rest of the population. Under apartheid, blacks were excluded from the "whites only" buses, "whites only" beaches, and "whites only" hospitals. Blacks could not run for office or live in a white neighborhood.

Apartheid legalized racism.

Mandela was the perfect man to challenge it. As a descendant of royalty, he was educated in the finest schools. As the son of a Christian mother, he embraced her love for God and people. Under the tutelage of a tribal chief, he learned the art of compromise and consensus. And as a young black lawyer in Cape Town, he experienced "a thousand slights, a thousand indignities, a thousand unremembered moments,"[27] which produced an inward fire to fight the system that imprisoned his people.

By the mid-1950s, Mandela was a force to be reckoned with. Passionate. Bitter. Given to retaliation. With his enviable pedigree and impressive stature (six feet two inches, 245 pounds), he was, for many, the hope of the black culture. But then came the events of August 5, 1962. Government officials arrested Mandela, convicted him of treason, and sent him to prison. For the next twenty-seven years, he stared through wired windows. And he wondered, surely he wondered, how a season in prison could play a part in God's plan.

You've asked such questions yourself. Perhaps not about time in prison but about your time in a dead-end job, struggling church, puny town, or enfeebled body. Certain elements of life make sense. But what about autism, Alzheimer's, or Mandela's prison sentence on Robben

Island? Was Paul including these conditions when he wrote Romans 8:28?

> And we know that in all things God works for the good of those who love him, who have been called according to his purpose.

We know . . . There are so many things we do not know. We do not know if the economy will dip or if our team will win. We do not know what our spouse is thinking or how our kids will turn out. We don't even know "what we ought to pray for" (Romans 8:26). But according to Paul, we can be absolutely certain about four things. We know . . .

1. *God works.* He is busy behind the scenes, above the fray, within the fury. He hasn't checked out or moved on. He is ceaseless and tireless. He never stops working.

2. *God works for the good.* Not for our comfort or pleasure or entertainment, but for our ultimate good. Since he is the ultimate good, would we expect anything less?

3. *God works for the good of those who love him.*

Behold the benefit of loving God! Make his story your story, and your story takes on a happy ending. Guaranteed. Being the author of our salvation, he writes a salvation theme into our biography.

4. *God works in all things.* *Panta,* in Greek. Like "*panoramic*" or "*panacea*" or "*pandemic.*" All-inclusive. God works, not through a few things or through the good things, best things, or easy things. But in "all things" God works.

Puppet in the hands of fortune or fate? Not you. You are in the hands of a living, loving God. Random collection of disconnected short stories? Far from it. Your life is a crafted narrative written by a good God, who is working toward your supreme good.

God is not slipshod or haphazard. He planned creation according to a calendar. He determined the details of salvation "before the foundation of the world" (1 Peter 1:20 NKJV). The death of Jesus was not an afterthought, nor was it Plan B or an emergency operation. Jesus died "when the set time had fully come" (Galatians 4:4), according to God's "deliberate plan and foreknowledge" (Acts 2:23).

God, in other words, isn't making up a plan as he goes along. Nor did he wind up the clock and walk away. "The Most High God rules the kingdom of mankind and sets over it whom he will" (Daniel 5:21 ESV). He "executes judgment, putting down one and lifting up another" (Psalm 75:7 ESV). "The LORD will not turn back until he has executed and accomplished the intentions of his mind" (Jeremiah 30:24 ESV). Look at those verbs: God *rules, sets, executes, accomplished.* These terms confirm the existence of heavenly blueprints and plans. Those plans include you. "In him we were also chosen, . . . according to the plan of him who works out everything in conformity with the purpose of his will" (Ephesians 1:11).

This discovery changes everything! It changed the outlook of the mom Denalyn and I visited in the maternity ward two days ago. She had miscarried a child. Her face awash with tears and heart heavy with questions, she reached through the fog and held on to God's hand. "This will work out for good, won't it, Max?" I assured her it would, and reminded her of God's promise: " 'For I know the plans I have for you,' declares the LORD, 'plans to prosper you and not to harm you, plans to give you hope and a future' " (Jeremiah 29:11).

The apostle Paul's life is proof. We know just enough of his story to see God's hand in each phase of it. Here is how Paul began his testimony: "I am indeed a Jew, born in Tarsus of Cilicia, but brought up in this city at the feet of

Gamaliel, taught according to the strictness of our fathers' law, and was zealous toward God as you all are today" (Acts 22:3 NKJV).

Paul grew up in Tarsus. He called it "an important city" (Acts 21:39 NLT). He wasn't exaggerating. Tarsus sat only a few miles from the coast and served as a hub for sailors, pirates, and merchants from all sections of Europe and Asia. Any child raised in Tarsus would have heard a dozen languages and witnessed a tapestry of cultures.

Tarsus was also a depot city on the Roman highway system. The empire boasted a network of roads that connected business centers of the ancient world. Ephesus. Iconium. Derbe. Syrian Antioch and Caesarea. While young Paul likely didn't visit these cities, he grew up hearing about them. Tarsus instilled a Mediterranean map in his heart and a keen intellect in his mind. Tarsus rivaled the academic seats of Alexandria and Athens. Paul conversed with students in the streets and, at the right age, became one himself. He learned the lingua franca of his day: Greek. He mastered it. He spoke it. He wrote it. He thought it.

Paul not only spoke the international language of the world; he carried its passport. He was born a Jew and a Roman citizen. Whenever he traveled through the empire, he was entitled to all the rights and privileges of a Roman citizen. He could enter any port and demand a judicial hearing. He could even appeal to Caesar. He was treated, not as a slave or foreigner, but as a freeman. How did his father acquire such a status? Perhaps in exchange for tents. Paul, himself a tentmaker, likely learned his craft from his father, who probably created durable gear for the ever-mobile Roman soldiers.

Young Paul left Tarsus with everything an itinerant missionary would need: cultural familiarity, linguistic skills, documents for travel, and a trade for earning a living. That was only the beginning.

Paul's parents sent him to Jerusalem for rabbinical studies. He memorized large sections of the Torah and digested massive amounts of rabbinical law. He was a valedictorian-level student, a Hebrew of Hebrews. Paul later wrote: "I was advancing in Judaism beyond many of my own age among my people, so extremely zealous was I for the traditions of my fathers" (Galatians 1:14 ESV).

An interesting side note. Paul and Jesus may have passed each other on the streets of Jerusalem. If Paul was a member of the Sanhedrin court when he persecuted the church, he would have been at least thirty years old, the minimum-age requirement for being a member of the court. That would make him roughly the same age as Jesus, who was crucified in his early thirties. Which raises this fanciful question: Did young Paul and young Jesus find themselves in Jerusalem at the same time? A twelve-year-old Messiah and his father. A young Saul and his studies. If so, did the Christ at some point cast a glance at his future apostle-to-be?

We know God did. Before Paul was following God, God was leading Paul. He gave him an education, a vocation, the necessary documentation. He schooled Paul in the law of Moses and the language of Greece. Who better to present Jesus as the fulfillment of the law than a scholar of the law?

But what about Paul's violence? He confessed: "I persecuted this Way to the death, binding and delivering into prisons both men and women" (Acts 22:4 NKJV). He tore husbands from their homes and moms from their children. He declared jihad against the church and spilled the blood of disciples. Could God use this ugly chapter to advance his cause?

More than a hypothetical question. We all have seasons that are hard to explain. Before we knew God's story, we made a mess of our own. Even afterward, we're prone to demand our own way, cut our own path, and hurt people in the process. Can God make good out of our bad?

He did with Paul.

"Now it happened, as I journeyed and came near Damascus at about noon, suddenly a great light from heaven shone around me. And I fell to the ground and heard a voice saying to me . . ."

ACTS 22:6–7 NKJV

"I'm going to give you a taste of your own medicine."
"Back to the dust with you, you Christian-killer."
"Prepare to meet your Maker!"

✤

Did Paul expect to hear words like these? Regardless, he didn't. Even before he requested mercy, he was offered mercy. Jesus told him:

"I have a job for you. I've handpicked you to be a servant and witness to what's happened today, and to what I am going to show you.

"I'm sending you off to open the eyes of the outsiders so they can see. . . . I'm sending you off to present my offer of sins forgiven, and a place in the family."

ACTS 26:16–18 MSG

Jesus transformed Paul, the card-carrying legalist, into a champion for mercy. Who would have thought? Yet who would be better qualified? Paul could write epistles of grace by dipping his pen into the inkwell of his own heart. He'd learned Greek in the schools of Tarsus, tentmaking in the home of his father, the Torah at the feet of Gamaliel. And he learned about love when Jesus paid him a personal visit on Damascus Highway.

"All things" worked together.

I saw an example of this process in our kitchen. My intent was to chat with Denalyn about some questions. She was stirring up a delicacy for someone's birthday. She assured me she could talk and bake at the same time. So I talked. She baked. But as she baked, I stopped talking.

Had I never witnessed the creation of cuisine? *Au contraire!* I've applauded the society of Julia Child since I was a child. We who do not cook stand in awe of those who do. And I did.

Denalyn buzzed about the kitchen like the queen of the hive. She snatched boxes off the shelves, pulled bowls out of the pantry. I've been known to stare at an open refrigerator for days in search of mayonnaise or ketchup. Not Denalyn. She grabbed the carton of eggs with one hand and butter with the other, never pausing to look.

She positioned the ingredients and utensils on the

table as a surgeon would her tools. Once everything was in place, off she went. Eggs cracking, yolks dropping. Shake this, stir that. Pour out the milk. Measure the sugar. Sift, mix, and beat. She was a blur of hands and elbows, a conductor of the kitchen, the Cleopatra of cuisine, the da Vinci of da kitchen, the lord of the lard, the boss of the bakery.

She popped the pan into the oven, turned the knob to 350 degrees, wiped her hands with a towel, turned to me, and said the words I longed to hear: "Want to lick the bowl?" I fell at her feet and called her blessed. Well, maybe not. But I did lick the bowl, spatula, and beaters. And I did wonder if Denalyn's work in the kitchen is a picture of God's work in us.

All the transfers, layoffs, breakdowns, breakups, and breakouts. Difficulties. Opportunities. Sifted and stirred and popped into the oven. Heaven knows, we've felt the heat. We've wondered if God's choice of ingredients will result in anything worth serving.

If Nelson Mandela did, no one could blame him. His prison life was harsh. He was confined to a six-by-six-foot concrete room. It had one small window that overlooked the courtyard. He had a desk, a mattress, a chair, three blankets, and a rusted-iron sanitary bucket for washing and shaving. Meals came from corn: breakfast was a porridge of corn scraped from the cob; lunch and sup-per consisted of corn on the cob; coffee was roasted corn mixed with water.

Mandela and the other prisoners were awakened at 5:30 a.m. They crushed rocks into gravel until noon, ate lunch, then worked until 4:00 p.m. Back in the cell at 5:00, asleep by 8:00. Discrimination continued even into the prison. Africans, like Mandela, were required to wear short pants and were denied bread.

Yet God used it all to shape Mandela. The prisoner read widely: Leo Tolstoy, John Steinbeck, Daphne du Maurier. He exercised daily: a hundred fingertip push-ups, two hundred sit-ups, fifty deep knee bends. Most of all he honed the capacity to compromise and forgive. He developed courtesy in all situations, disarming even the guards who had been placed to trouble him. He became particularly close to one jailer who, over two decades, read the Bible and discussed Scripture with Mandela. "'All men,' Mandela reflected later, 'have a core of decency, and … if their heart is touched, they are capable of changing.'"[28]

After twenty-seven years of confinement, at the age of seventy-two, Mandela was released. Those who knew him well described the pre-prison Mandela as "cocky and pugnacious." But the refined Mandela? "I came out mature," he said. He was devoted to "rationality, logic, and compromise." Journalists noted his lack of bitterness. Others observed that he was "unmarred by rancor."[29] Within four years Mandela was elected president and set out to lead South Africa out of apartheid and into a new era of equality.

God needed an educated, sophisticated leader who'd mastered the art of patience and compromise, so he tempered Mandela in prison.

He needed a culture-crossing, Greek-speaking, border-passing, Torah-quoting, self-supporting missionary, so he gave grace to Paul, and Paul shared grace with the world.

And you? In a moment before moments, your Maker looked into the future and foresaw the needs and demands of your generation. He instilled, and is instilling, within you everything you need to fulfill his plan in this era. "God made us to do good works, which God planned in advance for us to live our lives doing" (Ephesians 2:10 NCV).

If that doesn't take the cake, I don't know what does.

CHAPTER TEN

When You Discover Your Place in God's Plan ...

GOD WILL
COME FOR YOU

With hopes of earning extra cash, my dad once took a three-month job assignment in New England. I was ten years old, midway between training wheels and girlfriends. I thought much about baseball and bubble gum. Can't say I ever thought once about Bangor, Maine. Until Dad went there.

When he did, I found the town on the map. I calculated the distance between the Texas plains and the lobster coast. My teacher let me write a report on Henry Wadsworth Longfellow, and Dad sent us a jug of maple syrup. Our family lived in two worlds, ours and his.

We talked much about my father's pending return. "When Dad comes back, we will ... fix the basketball net ... take a trip to Grandma's ... stay up later." Mom used his coming to comfort and caution. She could do both with the same phrase. With soft assurance, "Your dad will be home soon." Or clenched teeth, "Your dad will be home soon." She circled his arrival date on the calendar and crossed out each day as it passed. She made it clear: Dad's coming would be a big deal.

It was. Four decades have weathered the memories, but these remain: the sudden smell of Old Spice in the house; his deep, bellowing voice; gifts all around; and a happy sense of settledness. Dad's return changed everything.

The return of Christ will do likewise.

Jude has a name for this event: "the great Day" (Jude 6).

The great Day will be a normal day. People will drink coffee, endure traffic snarls, laugh at jokes, and take note of the weather. Thousands of people will be born; thousands will die.

> The Arrival of the Son of Man will take place in times like Noah's. Before the great flood everyone was carrying on as usual, having a good time right up to the day Noah boarded the ark. They knew nothing—until the flood hit and swept everything away.
>
> MATTHEW 24:37–39 MSG

The tourists on Thailand's coast come to mind. They spent the morning of December 26, 2004, applying suntan lotion and throwing beach balls, unaware that a tsunami-stirred wave was moving toward them at the speed of a jetliner. Christ's coming will be equally unexpected. Most people will be oblivious, playing on the beach.

His shout will get our attention. "For the Lord Himself will descend from heaven with a shout" (1 Thessalonians 4:16 NKJV). Before we see angels, hear trumpets, or embrace our grandparents, we will be engulfed by Jesus' voice. John heard the voice of God and compared it to "the sound of many waters" (Revelation 1:15 NKJV). Perhaps you've stood at the base of a cataract so loud and full of fury that you had to shout to be heard. Or maybe you've heard the roar of a lion. When the king of beasts opens his mouth, every head in the jungle lifts. The King of kings will prompt the same response: "The Lord will roar from on high" (Jeremiah 25:30).

Lazarus heard such a roar. His body was entombed and his soul in paradise when Jesus shouted into both places: "[Jesus] cried with a loud voice, 'Lazarus, come forth!' And he who had died came out" (John 11:43–44 NKJV). Expect the same shout and shaking of the corpses on the great Day. "The dead will hear the voice of the Son of God. . . .

All who are ... in their graves will hear his voice. Then they will come out" (John 5:25, 28–29 NCV).

The shout of God will trigger the "voice of an archangel ... with the trumpet of God" (1 Thessalonians 4:16 NKJV). The archangel is the commanding officer. He will dispatch armies of angels to their greatest mission: to gather the children of God into one great assemblage. Envision these silvered messengers spilling out of the heavens into the atmosphere. You'll more quickly count the winter snowflakes than you will number these hosts. Jude announced that "the Lord is coming with thousands and thousands of holy angels to judge everyone" (verses 14–15 CEV). The population of God's armies was too high for John to count. He saw "ten thousand times ten thousand, and thousands of thousands" (Revelation 5:11 NKJV).

They minister to the saved and battle the devil. They keep you safe and clear your path. "He has put his angels in charge of you to watch over you wherever you go" (Psalm 91:11 NCV). And on the great Day, they will escort you into the skies, where you will meet God. "He'll dispatch the angels; they will pull in the chosen from the four winds, from pole to pole" (Mark 13:27 MSG).

Whether you are in Peoria or paradise, if you're a follower of Jesus, you can count on an angelic chaperone into the greatest gathering in history. We assume the demons will gather the rebellious. We aren't told. We are told, however, that the saved and lost alike will witness the assembly. "All the nations will be gathered before him" (Matthew 25:32).

The Population Reference Bureau estimates that 106 billion people have been born since the dawn of the human race.[30] Every single one of them will stand in the great assembly of souls. He who made us will convene us. "The LORD, who scattered his people, will gather them" (Jeremiah 31:10 NLT). "All the ends of the earth shall see the salvation of our God" (Isaiah 52:10 ESV).

At some point in this grand collection, our spirits will be reunited with our bodies:

> It will happen in a moment, in the blink of an eye, when the last trumpet is blown. For when the trumpet sounds, those who have died will be raised to live forever. And we who are living will also be transformed. For our dying bodies must be transformed into bodies that will never die; our mortal bodies must be transformed into immortal bodies.
>
> 1 CORINTHIANS 15:52–53 NLT

Paradise will give up her souls.

The earth will give up her dead, and the sky will stage a reunion of spirit and flesh. As our souls reenter our bodies, a massive sound will erupt around us: "On that day heaven will pass away with a roaring sound. Everything that makes up the universe will burn and be destroyed. The earth and everything that people have done on it will be exposed" (2 Peter 3:10 GWT).

Jesus called this "the re-creation of the world" (Matthew 19:28 MSG). God will purge every square inch that sin has contaminated, polluted, degraded, or defiled. But we may not even notice the reconstruction, for an even greater sight will appear before us: "the Son of Man coming on the clouds in the sky with power and great glory" (Matthew 24:30 GWT).

God has often used clouds to indicate his presence. He led the Israelites with a cloudy pillar. He spoke to Moses through the mist on Sinai, and to Jesus through the cloud at the transfiguration. Clouds symbolize his hiddenness, but on the great Day they will declare his visible presence. Note the preposition. "the Son of Man coming *on* the clouds" (emphasis mine). Subtle distinction. Great declaration. Every person, prince, pauper, saint, sinner—every eye will see Jesus. "All the nations will be gathered before him" (Matthew 25:32).

By this point we will have seen much: the flurry of

angels, the ascension of the bodies, the great gathering of the nations. We will have heard much: the shout of God and the angel, the trumpet blast, and the purging explosion. But every sight and sound will seem a remote memory compared to what will happen next: "He will be King and sit on his great throne" (Matthew 25:31 NCV).

This is the direction in which all of history is focused. This is the moment toward which God's plot is moving. The details, characters, antagonists, heroes, and subplots all arc in this direction. God's story carries us toward a coronation for which all creation groans:

> For everything, absolutely everything, above and below, visible and invisible, rank after rank after rank of angels—*everything* got started in him and finds its purpose in him.... He was supreme in the beginning and—leading the resurrection parade—he is supreme in the end.
>
> COLOSSIANS 1:16, 18 MSG

God's creation will return to its beginning: a one-king kingdom. Our earth is plagued by multiple competing monarchs, each one of us climbing ladders and claiming thrones. But we will gladly remove our crowns when Christ comes back for us.

During one of the crusades, Philippe Auguste, king of France, gathered his noble knights and men to call them to be strong in battle. He placed his crown on a table with the inscription "To the most worthy." He pledged the crown as the prize to be given to the bravest fighter.

They went to battle and returned victorious and encircled the table on which the crown had been placed. One of the nobles stepped forward, took the crown, and put it on the head of the king, saying, "Thou, O King, art the most worthy."[31]

On the great Day you'll hear billions of voices make the identical claim about Jesus Christ. "Every knee will bow to the name of Jesus—everyone in heaven, on earth, and under the earth. And everyone will confess that Jesus Christ is Lord" (Philippians 2:10–11 NCV).

Multitudes of people will bow low like a field of wind-blown wheat, each one saying, "Thou, O King, art the most worthy."

There will be one monumental difference. Some people will continue the confession they began on earth. They will crown Christ again, gladly. Others will crown him for the first time. They will do so sadly. They denied Christ on earth, so he will deny them in heaven.

But those who accepted him on earth will live with God forever. "I heard a voice thunder from the Throne:

'Look! Look! God has moved into the neighborhood, making his home with men and women! They're his people, he's their God'" (Revelation 21:3 MSG). The narrator makes the same point four times in four consecutive phrases:

"God has moved into the neighborhood"

"making his home with men and women"

"They're his people"

"he's their God"

The announcement comes with the energy of a six-year-old declaring the arrival of his father from a long trip. "Daddy's home! He's here! Mom, he's back!" One statement won't suffice. This is big news worthy of repetition. We shall finally see God face-to-face. "They will see his face" (Revelation 22:4).

Let this sink in. You will see the face of God. You will look into the eyes of the One who has always seen; you will behold the mouth that commands history. And if there is anything more amazing than the moment you see his face, it's the moment he touches yours. "He will wipe every tear from their eyes" (Revelation 21:4).

God will touch your tears. Not flex his muscles or

show off his power. Lesser kings would strut their stallions or give a victory speech. Not God. He prefers to rub a thumb across your cheek as if to say, "There, there ... no more tears."

Isn't that what a father does?

There was much I didn't understand about my father's time in Maine. The responsibilities of his job, his daily activities, the reason he needed to go. I was too young to comprehend all the details. But I knew this much: he would come home.

By the same token, who can understand what God is doing? These days on earth can seem so difficult: marred by conflict, saddened by separation. We fight, pollute, discriminate, and kill. Societies suffer from innumerable fiefdoms, small would-be dynasties. *What is this world coming to?* we wonder. God's answer: A great Day. On the great Day all of history will be consummated in Christ. He will assume his position "far above all rule and authority and power and dominion ... not only in this age but also in the one to come" (Ephesians 1:21 NASB). And he, the Author of it all, will close the book on this life and open the book to the next and begin to read to us from his unending story.

CONCLUSION

When You Discover Your Place in God's Plan ...

YOU WILL FINALLY GRADUATE

MAY 19, 2007, WAS A SPLENDID NIGHT FOR AN OUTDOOR graduation. The South Texas sky was as blue as a robin's egg. A just-passed rain shower perfumed the air. Thirty-four members of the Lucado clan occupied a sizable section of the amphitheater seats in honor of high-school-graduating Sara, my youngest daughter.

Never accused of timidity, we Lucados attempted to do the wave as Sara walked across the platform. We more closely resembled popping popcorn . . . but Sara heard our support. Graduation warrants such displays. There's nothing small about the transfer of tassels. Cut the cake and call the newspaper. Applaud the closing, not of a chapter, but of a tome. Graduation is no small matter.

What we didn't know, however, is that two Lucado

women were graduating the same evening. About the same time Sara stepped across the platform, my mom stepped into paradise. Sara and Thelma, separated in age by seventy-six years, yet joined by the same graduation date.

Applause for the first. Tears for the second. *Hooray* for Sara. *Oh, my* about Mom. Gladness. Sadness. The sorrow is understandable. Reactions to graduation and death shouldn't be identical.

Yet should they be so different?

Both celebrate completion and transition. And both gift the graduate with recognition: a diploma to one and a brand-new life to the other.

It will take only a second—as quickly as an eye blinks—when the last trumpet sounds. The trumpet will sound, and those who have died will be raised to live forever, and we will all be changed. This body that can be destroyed must clothe itself with something that can never be destroyed. And this body that dies must clothe itself with something that can never die.

1 CORINTHIANS 15:52–53 NCV

As you discover your place in God's plan, you make

this wonderful discovery: you will graduate from this life into heaven. Jesus' plan is to "gather together in one all things in Christ" (Ephesians 1:10 NKJV). "All things" includes your body. Your eyes that read this book. Your hands that hold it. Your blood-pumping heart, arm-hinging elbow, weight-supporting torso. God will reunite your body with your soul and create something unlike anything you have seen: an eternal body.

You will finally be healthy. You never have been. Even on the days you felt fine, you weren't. You were a sitting duck for disease, infections, airborne bacteria, and microbes. And what about you on your worst days?

Last Sunday as I sat in front of our church, my eyes seemed to radar toward the physically challenged. A recent retiree with a rush of white hair just found out about a brain tumor. So did a thirtyish mother of three. "I thought it was a migraine," she had told me earlier in the week.

Philip is in law school and a wheelchair. I haven't seen Adam in several weeks. He's a Juilliard grad. Multiple sclerosis has silenced his keyboard. Doctors are giving another member two months to live.

I hate disease. I'm sick of it.

So is Christ. Consider his response to the suffering of a deaf mute. "He took him aside from the multitude, and put His fingers in his ears, and He spat and touched his tongue. Then, looking up to heaven, He sighed, and said to him, 'Ephphatha,' that is, 'Be opened'" (Mark 7:33–34 NKJV).

Everything about this healing stands out. The way Jesus separates the man from the crowd. The tongue and ear touching. The presence of Aramaic in the Greek account. But it's the sigh that we notice. Jesus looked up to heaven and sighed. This is a sigh of sadness, a deep breath, and a heavenly glance that resolves, "It won't be this way for long."

Jesus will heal all who seek healing in him. There are no exceptions to this promise — no nuances, fine-print conditions, or caveats. To say some will be healed beyond the grave by no means diminishes the promise. The truth is this: "When Christ appears, *we shall be like him*, for we shall see him as he is" (1 John 3:2, emphasis mine).

"We shall be like him." Let every parent of a Down syndrome or wheelchair-bound child write these words on the bedroom wall. Let the disabled, infected, bedridden, and anemic put themselves to sleep with the promise "We shall be like him." Let amputees and the atrophied take this promise to heart: "We shall be like him." We shall graduate from this version of life into his likeness.

You'll have a spiritual body. In your current state,

your flesh battles your spirit. Your eyes look where they shouldn't. Your taste buds desire the wrong drinks. Your heart knows you shouldn't be anxious, but your mind still worries. Can't we relate to Paul's confession? "I truly delight in God's commands, but it's pretty obvious that not all of me joins in that delight. Parts of me covertly rebel, and just when I least expect it, they take charge" (Romans 7:22–23 MSG).

Your "parts" will no longer rebel in heaven. Your new body will be a spiritual body, with all members cooperating toward one end. Joni Eareckson Tada's words are powerful on this point. She has been confined to a wheelchair since the age of seventeen. Yet the greatest heavenly attraction for her is not new legs but a new soul.

I can't wait to be clothed in righteousness. Without a trace of sin. True, it will be wonderful to stand, stretch, and reach to the sky, but it will be more wonderful to offer praise that is pure. I won't be crippled by distractions. Disabled by insincerity. I won't be handicapped by a ho-hum halfheartedness. My heart will join with yours and bubble over with effervescent adoration. We will finally be able to fellowship fully with the Father and the Son.

For me, this will be the best part of heaven.[32]

In heaven "there shall be no more curse" (Revelation 22:3 NKJV). As much as we hate carcinomas and cardiac arrests, don't we hate sin even more? Cystic fibrosis steals breath, but selfishness and stinginess steal joy. Diabetes can ruin the system of a body, but deceit, denial, and distrust are ruining society.

Heaven, however, has scheduled a graduation. Sin will no longer be at war with our flesh. Eyes won't lust, thoughts won't wander, hands won't steal, our minds won't judge, appetites won't rage, and our tongues won't lie. We will be brand-new.

Some of you live in such road-weary bodies: knees ache, eyes dim, skin sags. Others exited the womb on an uphill ride. While I have no easy answers for your struggle, I implore you to see your challenge in the scope of God's story. View these days on earth as but the opening lines of his sweeping saga. Let's stand with Paul on the promise of eternity.

So we're not giving up. How could we! Even though on the outside it often looks like things are falling apart on us, on the inside, where God is making new life, not a day goes by without his unfolding grace. These hard times are small potatoes compared to the coming good times, the lavish celebration prepared for us. There's far more here than meets the eye. The things we see now are here today, gone tomorrow. But the things we can't see now will last forever.

2 CORINTHIANS 4:16–18 MSG

I write these words during the final hours of a two-week vacation. I've passed the last dozen days with my favorite people, my wife and daughters. We've watched the sun set, fish jump, and waves crash. We've laughed at old stories and made new memories. A trip for the ages.

At its inception, however, I got searched at airport security. I removed my shoes and handed my boarding pass to the official. He instructed me to step over to the side. I groaned as he waved his wand over my body. Why single me out? Isn't it enough that we have to plod barefoot through a scanner? Do they think I am a terrorist? You can tell that I don't like the moments at airport security. But as I remember this vacation, I won't reflect on its irritating inauguration. It was necessary but quickly lost in the splendor of the vacation.

You suppose we'll someday say the same words about this life? "Necessary but quickly lost in the splendor of

heaven." I have a hunch we will. We'll see death differ-
ently too. We'll remember the day we died with the same
fondness we remember graduation day.

By the way, if I graduate before you do, you'll see me
waiting for you. I'll be the one in the stands starting the
wave.

NOTES

1. Ted Gup, "Hard Times, a Helping Hand," *New York Times*, December 22, 2008, www.nytimes.com/2008/12/22/opinion/22gup.html (September 27, 2010).

2. Cited in Richard Mayhue, *Unmasking Satan: Understanding Satan's Battle Plan and Biblical Strategies for Fighting Back* (Grand Rapids: Kregel, 2001), 22.

3. Martin Luther, "A Mighty Fortress Is Our God" (1529), *Lyrics Era*: www.lyricsera.com/433137-lyric-Religious+Music-A+Mighty+Fortress+Is+Our+God.html (October 1, 2010).

4. See A. E. Le Roy, "The Great Barrier Island," in *Journal of the Auckland-Waikato Historical Societies* (April 1978), *Great Barrier Island Tourist Directory*: www.thebarrier.co.nz/History/AELeRoy.htm (October 1, 2010).

5. See Charles Walcott, "Magnetic Orientation in Homing Pigeons," in *IEEE Transactions on Magnetics* 16 (September 1980): 1008–13, *IEEEXplore*: ieeexplore.ieee.org/xpl/freeabs_all.jsp?arnumber=1060868 (October 1, 2010).

6. Cited in John Gilmore, *Probing Heaven* (Grand Rapids: Baker, 1989), 65.

7. Paul Stokes, "Blinded Pilot Guided to Safe Landing by RAF" (© Telegraph Media Group Limited 2008; used by permission), *Telegraph.co.uk* (November 7, 2008), www.telegraph.co.uk/news/newstopics/howaboutthat/3400429/Blinded-pilot-guided-to-safe-landing-by-RAF.html (October 1, 2010).

8. "Sweat Lodge Death Investigation Turns to Self-Help Guru James Arthur Ray" (October 12, 2009), *CBS News*: www.cbsnews.com/8301-504083_162-5378668-504083.html (September 14, 2010); Mike Fleeman, "James Arthur Ray arrested in Sweat Lodge Deaths" (February 3, 2010), *People*: www.people.com/article/0,,20341429,00.html (September 14, 2010).

9. In the NIV, "Son of Man" appears eighty-two times in the Gospels. In Luke 24:7 the angels use the term to refer to Jesus, and in John 12:34 the crowd quotes Jesus describing himself as the Son of Man and asks what the name means. Twice in Mark's narrative (8:31; 9:9), Mark uses the term in paraphrasing Jesus' words.

10. John 8:12; 6:35; 11:25; 14:6 (NKJV); 8:58.

11. James Stalker, *The Life of Christ* (1880; repr., Arlington Heights, Ill.: Christian Liberty, 2002), 82.

12. Quoted in J. John and Chris Walley, *The Life: A Portrait of Jesus* (Milton Keynes, UK: Authentic Media, 2003), 126.

13. "Blind pilot guided to land by RAF" (November 7, 2010), *BBC News*: news.bbc.co.uk/2/hi/uk_news/england /north_yorkshire/7715345.stm; the audio account is embedded in the article (September 14, 2010).

14. "Tennessee Drunk Driving Laws," *Edgar Snyder & Associates*, www.edgarsnyder.com/drunk-driving/statute -limitations/tennessee-drunk-driving-laws.html (September 14, 2010).

15. Cited in Bryan Chapell, *The Promises of Grace: Living in the Grip of God's Love* (1992; repr., Grand Rapids: Baker, 2001), 142. Note: This report was disputed by some authorities.

16. Martin Luther, quoted in Donald G. Bloesch, *Essentials of Evangelical Theology* (San Francisco: HarperSanFrancisco, 1978), 1:148.

17. The story is told in Jon Krakauer, *Into the Wild* (New York: Anchor, 1996), 80–84.

18. Fred Carl Kuehner, "Heaven or Hell," in *Fundamentals of the Faith*, ed. Carl F. H. Henry (Grand Rapids: Zondervan, 1969), 233.

19. Based on mortality rates from "The World Factbook," last updated September 29, 2010, *Central Intelligence Agency*: www.cia.gov/library/publications/the-world-factbook/geos/xx.html (October 1, 2010). The figures are based on estimates of 8.37 deaths per 1,000 population (2009 estimate) and a world population of 6,768,181,146 (July 2010 estimate).

20. Mark 9:31 NKJV; see also 8:31; 10:33–34; 14:28

21. "Theology: The God Is Dead Movement" (October 25, 1965), *Time*: www.time.com/time/magazine/article/0,9171,941410–3,00.html (September 14, 2010).

22. Chaz Corzine, e-mail message to author, August 3, 2010. Used by permission.

23. Billy Graham, "Remarks by Dr. Billy Graham at Richard Nixon's Funeral" (April 27, 1994), *Watergate.info*: www.watergate.info/nixon/94-04-27_funeral-graham.shtml (September 14, 2010).

24. Cited in Jeff Strite, "The Power of Persistent Prayer," *SermonCentral.com*: www.sermoncentral.com/sermons/the-power-of-persistent-prayer-jeff-strite-sermon-on-prayer-how-to-49222.asp (September 14, 2010).

25. Mark Schlabach, "Injury Swipes McCoy's One Goal" (January 7, 2010), *ESPN*: sports.espn.go.com/ncf/bowls09/columns/story?columnist=schlabach_mark&id=4807219 (September 15, 2010); "Colt McCoy Postgame Interview

Video: 'I Would Have Given Everything to Be Out There'" (March 18, 2010), *The Huffington Post*: www .huffingtonpost.com/2010/01/08/colt-mccoy-postgame -inter_n_415841.html (October 1, 2010).

26. Edward Mote, "My Hope Is Built on Nothing Less" (1834), *Hymns*: www.hymns.me.uk/my-hope-is-built-on -nothing-less-favorite-hymn.htm (October 28, 2010); put to music in 1863 by composer William Bradbury.

27. David Aikman, *Great Souls: Six Who Changed the Century* (Nashville: Word, 1998), 78. Many of the details of Mandela's life described in this chapter are taken from pages 61–123 of *Great Souls*.

28. Aikman, *Great Souls*, 108.

29. Aikman, *Great Souls*, 116, 64.

30. Figures vary widely. The figure 106 billion is cited by Carl Haub, "How Many People Have Ever Lived on Earth" (November/December 2002), *Population Reference Bureau*: www.prb.org/Articles/2002/HowMany PeopleHaveEverLivedonEarth.aspx (October 1, 2010).

31. Cited in Paul Lee Tan, *Encyclopedia of 7700 Illustrations: Signs of the Times* (Rockville, Md.: Assurance, 1988), #5470.

32. Joni Eareckson Tada, *Heaven: Your Real Home* (Grand Rapids: Zondervan, 1995), 41.

MORE

to

YOUR

STORY

PARTICIPANT'S GUIDE

Prepared by Kevin and Sherry Harney

WHEN YOU DISCOVER YOUR PLACE IN GOD'S PLAN

God's story is glorious,
surprising, victorious, and beautiful.
His story, when we really listen closely,
is our story.

INTRODUCTION

Do you remember a time you got lost? Perhaps it was a crowded day at the mall, and you wandered away from Dad and Mom for just a moment, and they were gone. You felt the paralyzing fear of looking around and failing to see the north star of your parents' strong presence. You were lost.

Maybe it was a school trip to the zoo and you inadvertently lingered at the monkey cage while the rest of the class moved on. Before you knew it, you were alone. People were everywhere, but not a face in the crowd was familiar. Lost!

It might have been a drive late at night, and a wrong turn spun you around, and, truth be known, you had no idea where to go next.

These moments of lostness can leave a pit in your stomach and bring fear to your soul ... until the store clerk finds your parents, your teacher taps you on the shoulder and says, "Keep up with the class," or a gas station attendant pulls out a map and shows you how to get back on the interstate.

> *Above and around us God directs a grander saga, written by his hand, orchestrated by his will, unveiled according to his calendar. And you are a part of it.*
>
> —MAX LUCADO

What is even worse is coming to a point in life when we realize that we have lost our way as a human being. We might know our mailing address and how to get to school, work, or church, but we are not sure why we are on this planet. We have no sense of our purpose.

It is in these moments that we look to God, the Master Story-teller, and discover that the best way to understand our story is to listen to his. As we understand God's story and where we fit within it, the haze begins to clear and our story begins to make sense.

TALK ABOUT IT

Tell about a time in your childhood when you got lost and how you felt when you were finally found.

DVD TEACHING NOTES

As you watch the video teaching segment for session 1, featuring Max Lucado, use the following outline to record anything that stands out to you.

An uninformed Munchkin

When everything changes

Getting lost in Grandma's story

What knowing does to us

Knowing God's story

The central message of God's story

Your story indwells God's story

> *Everything changes when you know the rest of your story.*
> —MAX LUCADO

DVD DISCUSSION

1. Share about a time when someone told you about your family history and certain things about you and your family members began to make sense.

2. Tell about a time you were reading the Bible (God's story) and a light went on in your heart as you realized that this was really your story.

3. If the story of the Bible is going to make sense, it is important to know how it begins and how it ends. In your own words, how does the Bible begin? What are the epic themes that launch us into the story of the Bible (Genesis)?

In your own words, how does the Bible end? What are the epic themes that conclude the story of the Bible (Revelation)?

4. How does your family history help you have a sense of who you are and where your life is going? How does knowing the story of God's family in the Bible help you know who you are and where you are going?

> *God wants you to know his story. Knowing connects us,*
> *links us, bonds us to something greater than we are. Knowing*
> *reminds us that we aren't floating on isolated ponds but on a*
> *grand river.*
>
> —MAX LUCADO

5. Max talked about being dropped into Munchkin Land and being very confused because he did not actually know the storyline of *The Wizard of Oz.* How can reading the Bible without any context or background become a frustrating or dangerous enterprise?

6. What is one of your favorite stories in the Bible and how do you see yourself and your personal story informed by this portion of God's Word?

7. **Read:** John 3:16–17. In the video, Max said that this portion of God's story contains one of the central messages of the Bible. What core messages do you find in this passage?

How can these messages help us understand who we are and how we are to live in this journey through life?

8. **Read:** Ephesians 1:11–14. How do you see God's story and our story woven together in this passage of the Bible?

> *Your story indwells God's. This is the great promise of the Bible.*
>
> —MAX LUCADO

9. What approach to learning God's Word has most helped you dig in and grow in your love for the Bible?

10. How can your group members pray for you, encourage you, and keep you accountable in reading the Bible and seeking to know God's story in greater depth?

CLOSING PRAYER

Take time as a group to pray in some of the following directions:

- Thank God for his Word, the Bible. Ask him to help you know and love his Word so that you may grow to see your story woven into his story.

- Pray for people you care about who are wandering and lost because they do not know God's story.

- Confess where you have avoided or neglected digging into God's story in the Bible. Pray for a renewed commitment to read and study the Scriptures with fresh passion.

- Lift up group members who have shared a desire to grow in their knowledge of and love for God's Word. Pray that they will take the steps needed, and exercise the discipline required, to go deep into the truth of the Bible.

> *Your life emerges from the greatest mind and the kindest heart in the history of the universe: the mind and heart of God.*
>
> —MAX LUCADO

BETWEEN SESSIONS

Personal Reflection

Take time to think through three or four of your favorite stories in the Bible. Why are you drawn to these stories? How do you see your story connected to these stories? How did God work in these accounts and what are ways you have seen God work in similar ways in your life?

Personal Action

Contact a patriarch or matriarch in your family and ask if you can spend time with them, face to face or over the phone. Ask questions about your family, their life, and those who have gone before you. Listen with an open heart and seek to discover more about what has formed you and those you love.

Group Engagement

Consider inviting each group member to make a personal commitment to read and reflect on the Bible in the weeks your group meets. Don't have a required reading plan, but have each person set a personal goal. Then, when you meet, ask every person to tell about how they are doing in meeting their own goal and, if possible, to share one lesson they learned in their reading and how it impacts and informs their personal story.

Name: *Personal Goal:*

_____

_____

_____

_____

_____

_____

_____

_____

_____

_____

_____

_____

_____

_____

_____

_____

_____

_____

ORDINARY MATTERS

*Our world praises and exalts the "extraordinary";
God meets normal people in the ordinary places of life.*

INTRODUCTION

Have you ever seen the motivational posters that grace the walls of so many office buildings? One poster features a crew in a rowboat straining together, the word "TEAMWORK" emblazoned under the photo. Another boasts a stunning ocean shoreline with an enormous rock formation thrusting heavenward from the water. Beneath the picture is the word "INTEGRITY" and the caption, "Do what you know is right ... always. With commitment to your deepest convictions you stand tall against time and tide."

In response to such highly optimistic and cheerful messages, another company, Despair.com, has begun to make its own line of posters. One poster, titled "CONFORMITY," shows a large herd of zebras and the caption, "When people are free to do as they please, they usually imitate each other." Another poster, titled "INDIVIDU-ALITY," shows beautiful snowflakes float-ing in the air and text that reads, "Always remember that you are unique. Just like everybody else."

The irony of these two competing com-panies is that one makes a lot of money selling posters designed to make people feel

> God writes his story with people like Joseph and Mary ... and you!
>
> —MAX LUCADO

special. The other makes a lot of money helping people laugh at that fact that most of us are really quite ordinary and common.

When we read the story of God's people in the Bible we discover that most of them are more like us than we would have guessed. The vast majority of stories in the Bible introduce us to folks that are more ordinary than extraordinary.

TALK ABOUT IT

Who is a person in the Bible (Jesus excluded) whom you find very interesting? What is one way this person seems a lot like you ... normal?

DVD TEACHING NOTES

As you watch the video teaching segment for session 2, featuring Max Lucado, use the following outline to record anything that stands out to you.

A children's Christmas play

God inside a girl

Jesus' birth drips with normalcy

Our everyday life: Norm and Norma

Jesus' connection to the dawn of time

The Word become flesh

Jesus "dwelt" among us

> *The baby Mary held was connected to the dawn of time. He saw the first ray of sun and heard the first crash of a wave. The baby was born, but the Word never was.*
>
> —MAX LUCADO

DVD DISCUSSION

1. In our culture we tend to ignore the normal and ordinary and lift up the unique and extraordinary. Why do you think we do this and why might it be a dangerous way to live?

2. **Read:** Luke 2:1–7. God chose Joseph, an ordinary carpenter, to be the stepfather of Jesus, and Mary, a common peasant girl, to be the mother of God incarnate. As this Jewish couple came to Bethlehem for the census, what would people have seen by looking at them? How might people have responded if Joseph tried to tell them who Mary was and the true identity of the baby in her womb?

> *The story of Jesus' birth drips with normalcy. Normal has calluses like Joseph, stretch marks like Mary. Normal stays up late with laundry and wakes up early for work. Normal drives carpool wearing a bathrobe and slippers. Normal is Norm and Norma, not Prince and Princess.*
>
> —MAX LUCADO

3. In the video Max said, "The Christmas hope is that God indwells the everydayness of our world." What is one way you experience the presence and hope of God as you walk through a normal day?

4. God uses normal people such as Mary and Joseph to accomplish his will in this world. What is one way God has worked through your normal life in a way that is surprising and exciting for you?

5. If we are not careful, even in the church we can make people feel ordinary and unimportant. How can we make the people in our

church feel loved and welcomed? What can we do to reach out to those who are visiting our church for the first time to ensure that they feel embraced and wanted?

6. **Read:** John 1:1 – 3; Genesis 1:1 – 2; and Colossians 1:15 – 16. What do you learn about Jesus in these passages? In light of who Jesus really is, why is his humble birth so surprising and shocking?

> *The Word of God entered the world with the cry of a baby. Jesus, the Maker of the universe, the one who invented time and created breath, was born into a family too humble to swing a bed for a pregnant mom-to-be.*
>
> —MAX LUCADO

7. In the video, Max made this provocative statement, "The splendor of the first Christmas is the lack thereof." What do you think he is getting at?

8. Jesus came as one of us; he pitched his tent in an ordinary neighborhood. How can we be the presence of Jesus right where God has placed us?

9. Tell about an ordinary person that God used to write his story in your life. How is your life richer because of this person?

10. Consider someone God has placed in your life whom you might influence for him. How does God want to use you to help write

his story in their life? How can your group members encourage you and cheer you on in your effort?

CLOSING PRAYER

Take time as a group to pray in some of the following directions:

- Thank God that he came among us not as royalty, but as a normal person.

- Ask God to help you enter your neighborhood, workplace, social settings, wherever, as an ordinary person carrying the extraordinary love of Jesus.

- Pray for your church to have a welcoming heart that embraces common people. Pray against any spirit of elitism that might creep into your church.

- Pray for the presence of God's Holy Spirit to be so welcome in your heart and home that other people actually notice something different about you.

> *God became an embryo and indwelt the belly of a village girl. Christ in Mary. God in Christ.*
>
> —MAX LUCADO

BETWEEN SESSIONS

Personal Reflection

Think about how you can notice the presence of God in the flow of your normal day. Also, reflect on ways you can bring the presence of God in organic and natural ways into every part of your day. Invite Jesus to shine in and through you so that others will see his presence and want to know him.

Personal Action

Examine your heart. If you are guilty of adopting attitudes or actions that set you above and apart from others with a spirit of elitism, confess this to God and pray for a new attitude of humility and love for others.

Group Engagement

Consider having your group members commit to make a point of greeting one new person every Sunday for the coming month. If you don't see anyone new, be sure to welcome a person you don't know very well. Seek to make people feel welcomed and embraced.

YOU HEAR A VOICE YOU CAN TRUST

*In a world of voices crying
for our attention,
there is one that we must learn
to hear with crystal clarity.*

INTRODUCTION

In 1971 the Canadian rock group, Five Man Electrical Band, wrote a song that hit number three on the U.S. *Billboard* "Hot 100" and sold over a million copies. You might remember "Signs"—especially the catchy refrain:

> *Sign, sign, everywhere a sign*
> *Blocking out the scenery, breaking my mind*
> *Do this, don't do that, can't you read the sign?*

Throughout the song, a man expresses his frustration with all the signs (voices) telling him what to do or not to do. One voice says that he can't get a job at a local business if he is one of those "long-haired freaky people." Another lets him know he will be shot if he trespasses on private property. Still another informs him that the way he dresses and the fact that he does not have a membership card prohibits his inclusion in a private club.

In the final verse, he sees a sign on a church that says, "Everybody welcome, come in, kneel down, and pray," and he goes inside. When the offering plate comes by, he has no money so he writes his own little sign, his personal message to God: "Thank you, Lord, for thinking about me; I'm alive and doing fine."

All through time human beings have faced the challenge of learning to hear and recognize the voice of the one true God through the clutter of culture, societal messages, competing religious traditions, and the general noise of life's traffic. Many signs, messages, and voices seem to battle for our attention. If we are not careful, we can listen to the wrong voice, follow the wrong sign, and end up headed down a wrong road or even driving off a cliff.

> *Some believe that Jesus masterminded the greatest scheme in the history of humanity, that he out-Ponzied the swindlers and outhustled the hucksters. If that were true, billions of humans have been fleeced into following a first-century pied piper over the edge of a cliff.*
>
> —MAX LUCADO

TALK ABOUT IT

What are some of the big messages being declared in culture today and what are some possible consequences if we embrace and follow them?

DVD TEACHING NOTES

As you watch the video teaching segment for session 3, featuring Max Lucado, use the following outline to record anything that stands out to you.

Flying blind

Many voices

Jesus' important question

Peter's reply

Jesus' claims about himself

Jesus' impact on others

Wonderful truth about Jesus

DVD DISCUSSION

1. What are some ways Jesus comes alongside of us during our dark times to give direction and hope when we can't see what lies ahead?

2. Describe a person who has functioned as a wise, godly voice speaking into your life in both good and hard times. How has God used this person to give direction and provide safety on your journey?

3. When Jim O'Neill realized he was flying blind, he sent out a Mayday distress call. Tell about a time you cried out to God with a Mayday prayer and how he answered and came to your side.

4. What is an area of your life, right now, where you feel like you are flying blind? How can your group members pray for you and fly at your side during this challenging time?

5. What competing voices in your life are calling for your attention and distracting you from hearing the voice of Jesus? What can you do to minimize the volume of these voices to better hear the voice of Jesus?

6. **Read:** Mark 8:27–30. People in Jesus' day had all kinds of theories about who Jesus was. What were some of these theories and how would the people have been impacted if they believed these inaccurate voices?

> *Had Jesus been a fraud or trickster, the first Christian congregation would have died a stillborn death. People would have denounced the miracles of Christ. But they did just the opposite. They believed in them . . . and him!*
>
> —MAX LUCADO

7. Peter was the only disciple to give a clear and confident declaration of who Jesus was (and for the record . . . he was right!). Tell about a time in your life when the reality that Jesus is Messiah, Savior, and Lord became very real and personal for you. How did this awareness impact your ability to hear and follow the voice of Jesus?

8. **Read:** Matthew 9:4–7; 11:11; 12:6–8; 28:18–19; John 4:12–14; and 14:13–14. Some people like to say, "Jesus was a decent fellow, a great teacher, a wonderful moral person, but nothing more." In light of these passages, what do we learn about Jesus that shows he was far more than just a good person?

9. One of the ways we can see the truth of a person's message is the fruit that it bears. What are some of the ways the world has been made a better place because of the life and teaching of Jesus carried on by his followers? What are one or two ways your life has been made better because you have a relationship with Jesus?

> *Jesus transformed common dockworkers and net casters into the authors of history's greatest book and founders of its greatest movement.*
>
> —MAX LUCADO

10. Jesus is exactly who Peter declared him to be—the Savior who is with us at all times. What practical steps can you take to stay connected with Jesus throughout your day? How can you listen for his voice in dark times as well as times when things are going great?

CLOSING PRAYER

Take time as a group to pray in some of the following directions:

- Pray for ears to hear the loving, clear voice of Jesus speaking through the Word and by the Holy Spirit as you walk through your days.

- Ask God to give you and your group members discerning hearts and attentive ears to identify the false voices that speak in our world and wisdom to reject the messages that are contrary to God's Word and truth.

- Confess where you have been drawn into listening to unhealthy voices and ask God to help you shut off the source of false messages.

- Thank God for speaking through his Word, both written and incarnate.

What if Jesus really was, and is, the Son of God? If so, then we can relish this wonderful truth: we never travel alone. We do not know what the future holds. But we are not alone.

—MAX LUCADO

BETWEEN SESSIONS

Personal Reflection

Many voices cry out for our attention. Make a list of some of the unhealthy voices and sources of information that flow into your life:

Now make a list of the sources of healthy and Christ-honoring information that can impact your life:

Think and pray about practical ways you can turn down the volume of the unhealthy voices and increase your openness to the positive sources.

Personal Action

With the flood of voices screaming in our hearts and grabbing for our attention, it is always safe to listen to Jesus. During the coming month read the Gospels (Matthew, Mark, Luke, and John). Pay special attention to the words and teachings of Jesus. Let these become the filter you use to determine what other voices are worth hearing.

Group Engagement

One way to increase our learning and open our ears more to the voice of Jesus is sharing what we are learning from our personal study of God's Word. We can never go wrong when we read the Bible and listen for the voice of the Holy Spirit. Commit to share via email one or two things God is teaching you in his Word each week for the coming month. This way, you will all learn from each other and increase your ability to hear the truth of God.

YOU WON'T BE FORSAKEN

In Christ, all of our sins and wrongs can be washed away, as if they never existed.

INTRODUCTION

Where in the world do we get the idea that we have to work to prove we are worthy? At what point in our existence do we start feeling judged, graded, and measured on how we perform? What makes us feel like we must make restitution for our wrongs or we will never be acceptable?

Sadly, the tests and measurements begin with our first breath and cry as we leave the womb. A doctor or nurse plops us on a scale and weighs us like a trout fresh out of water. We are measured for length and our skin tone is assessed. Every baby is given an APGAR score within minutes of birth. Of course, this is not an official competition, but the measurements do matter to parents.

We praise, celebrate, and measure almost everything: the age a child rolls over, uses a potty chair, walks, talks, reads, and rides a bike. We give stars on charts in Sunday school for attendance, Bible memory verses, and bringing a Bible to church. As soon as a child can toddle we put them in cute little cleats and usher them onto a sports field and teach them how to win. As soon as school starts, children get checks and minuses and, later, years of report cards. When we enter the world of employment, yearly evaluations and raises (or no raises) tell us what our boss thinks we are worth.

Where do we get this strange notion that we must perform, work for what we have, and measure up? The answer is quite simple: it is drilled into our emotional DNA every day of our life. Do poorly ... pay the price! Behave well ... get praised! Drop the ball ... lose your spot on first string. Get good grades ... promises of scholarships come in the mail.

Into our orderly and consistent program of cause and effect steps Jesus. But he does not play by our rules. He disrupts the whole system. Jesus turns it all upside down and inside out. And when we get to know how Jesus does things ... a new life begins.

> *Jesus' sacrifice is a sufficient one. Our merits don't enhance it. Our stumbles don't diminish it. The sacrifice of Christ is a total and unceasing and accomplished work.*
>
> —MAX LUCADO

TALK ABOUT IT

Tell about a moment that occurred as you were growing up when you realized so much of life is based on how you perform and how hard you work.

DVD TEACHING NOTES

As you watch the video teaching segment for session 4, featuring Max Lucado, use the following outline to record anything that stands out to you.

The vest system

Our attempts to work ourselves out of our vests

Focus of the cross

Jesus forsaken

Christ dressed in our vests

Christ's sufficient sacrifice: the removal of our vests

Our new wardrobe

> *God does not simply remove our failures; he dresses us in the goodness of Christ! "For all of you who were baptized into Christ have clothed yourselves with Christ" (Galatians 3:27).*
>
> —MAX LUCADO

DVD DISCUSSION

1. Often we try to remove our vests of past shame and poor choices by doing good works. What are some of the ways we try to "work off" our vests and what are some problems with this approach?

2. Max pointed out that the Bible does not tell stories about how to work off our vests of shame. Rather, it offers accounts of how God's story redeems our story. What is a Bible passage or story that you like because it paints a picture of God's redemption and love for us, in spite of our sin and brokenness?

3. Without using names or details, tell about a time when someone confessed to you that they were wearing a vest of sin and shame. What counsel did you give them after they acknowledged their struggle?

4. If you are still wearing a vest of sin and shame, share its nature (if you're comfortable doing so) and why you have a hard time taking it off and giving it to Jesus. How can your group members pray for you as you seek to remove this vest?

5. **Read:** Matthew 27:32–56. According to the Gospels and the rest of the Bible, what did Jesus do to remove our vests and set us free from shame? What did the Father do in this process of offering us cleansing and freedom?

> *Jesus' death on the cross is not a secondary theme in Scripture; it is the core.*
>
> —MAX LUCADO

6. **Read:** 2 Corinthians 5:21; Isaiah 53:3–7; Galatians 3:13; and Romans 5:6–8. How did Jesus take our sins (vests of shame) on himself? How does this affect the way God sees us and the way we should see ourselves?

7. Though disputed by some, the story of Flight 255 is a compelling picture of a mother apparently wrapping herself around her daughter to take the impact of the fall and save her daughter's life. How does this story capture the love and grace of Jesus and what he did for us on the cross?

8. Picture Jesus on the cross and all of your sins (vests) and the judgment for them being placed on him. What would you say to Jesus if he were here right now and you could thank him for taking all your sin and shame on himself as he suffered and died on the cross?

> *When you make God's story yours, he covers you in Christ.*
> —MAX LUCADO

9. **Read:** 1 Peter 2:24 and 2 Corinthians 5:21. In the video, Max talked about the "Great Exchange" that happened on the cross. Our sins became Christ's and he bore them. His righteousness has become ours and we wear it like a beautiful new vest. How have you experienced the righteousness of Christ transforming your heart and life since becoming a follower of Jesus?

10. **Read:** 1 Peter 2:9–10; 2 Corinthians 6:1; 1 Corinthians 3:16–17; and Ephesians 2:10. When we receive Jesus and let him remove our vests of sin and shame, he gives us a new identity. Who do we become when we follow Jesus and let him give us a new life and future? How does our knowledge of our new identity send us into a whole new future?

CLOSING PRAYER

Take time as a group to pray in some of the following directions:

- Thank the Father for sending his own Son to die in your place and for your sins. Give praise to the Holy Spirit for drawing you to the heart of Jesus. Thank Jesus for paying the price to remove your vests, be cleansed of sin, and walk in freedom.

- Thank God for clothing you in his righteousness and pray for power to walk in this new life he offers.

- Ask God to give you boldness and clarity of mind as you seek to share the story of his grace and Jesus' sacrifice with family and friends who have not yet received this gift.

- Confess where you are still wearing vests of shame and ask for courage to place them at the foot of the cross.

> *Headline this truth: When God sees you, he sees his Son, not your sin. God "blots out your transgressions" and "remembers your sins no more" (Isaiah 43:25). No probation. No exception. No reversals.*
>
> —MAX LUCADO

BETWEEN SESSIONS

Personal Reflection

Read: Matthew 28:16–20 and 1 Peter 3:15. We are called to share the story of Jesus and give witness to what God has done in us. What might you say to *one* of these people if they were open to hear about your relationship with Jesus:

- A Christian friend who keeps putting on the same old vest of shame and guilt

- A non-Christian friend who does not believe God wants to forgive his past and give him a new future

- A teenager who grew up in the church but has never really understood God's love and grace

- A grade-school girl who wonders if there is a God out there who cares about her

Personal Action

Make a list of any vests you seem to keep taking back and wanting to wear again. Ask God for such a deep understanding of the sacrifice of Jesus that you will never wear these again.

Group Engagement

Over the coming month, be sure to ask a number of your group members these two questions:

Are you making sure you never wear your old vests of shame over past sin?

Are you proudly wearing the garments Jesus has placed on you?

YOUR FINAL CHAPTER BECOMES A PREFACE

In life, the end is often exactly that, the end.
With Jesus, the end can become the beginning.

INTRODUCTION

Most of us have attended a funeral or stood at the graveside of a person we truly loved. Moments like these are sobering, with a sense of finality that we tend to avoid in our day-to-day life. We face a spectrum of emotions that are deep and hard to put into words.

One moment we are thinking about how we will miss them. Our mind wanders to all they meant to us and how our life will be different without them ... tears flow.

The next moment we are talking with someone about how precious this person was to us and we recount a moment of intense joy and delight that we shared with them ... we smile and even laugh.

Five minutes later our mind wanders forward to the coming year as we seek to imagine Christmas, a birthday, or Valentine's Day without them ... and our heart grows heavy.

Up and down we go, like a child on a teeter-totter. Joy and sorrow. Tears and laughter. Highs and lows. This is the journey we travel when a loved one dies. Even Jesus wept at the tomb of Lazarus (John 11:35).

But covering the whole experience is a profound certainty and awareness that, if our loved ones were Christians, we will see them again. This is not the end of the story. God has already won. Death can't hold them. Jesus is on the throne ... risen and glorious. The grave is not their final destination; heaven is their home ... and ours as well.

> *The bodily resurrection means everything. If Jesus lives on only in spirit and deeds, he is but one of a thousand dead heroes. But if he lives on in flesh and bone, he is the King who pressed his heel against the head of death.*
>
> —MAX LUCADO

TALK ABOUT IT

Tell about a time that a Christian family member or friend passed away. What feelings did you have during this season of loss and how did you experience both sorrow and joy?

DVD TEACHING NOTES

As you watch the video teaching segment for session 5, featuring Max Lucado, use the following outline to record anything that stands out to you.

The folly of not having an exit strategy

No dream of a Sunday morning miracle

Plans to embalm Jesus, not talk to him

Cadaver turned King: he is risen!

The bodily resurrection of Jesus means everything

Promise about our grave

Death is not the final chapter

"He has risen." *Three words in English. Just one in Greek. Egerthe. So much rests on the validity of this one word. If it is false, then the whole of Christianity collapses like a poorly told joke. Yet, if it is true, then God's story has turned your final chapter into a preface.*

—MAX LUCADO

DVD DISCUSSION

1. We live in a day and age when many people don't look farther down the road than *today* or maybe *this weekend*. Carl McCunn's journal included these fateful words: "I think I should have used more foresight about arranging my departure." Why do so many people walk through this life failing to plan for their ultimate departure? What do Christians have to share with others that will help them get ready for the end of life on this planet?

2. Satan would love to keep every man, woman, and child so distracted and busy that they never face their own mortality and the reality that death looms in front of us all. What are some of the Enemy's distractions that keep people from asking important spiritual and eternal questions?

3. If a non-Christian friend or family member asked you, "What do you believe will happen to you when this life ends?" how would you explain eternity and your faith and confidence in God in a way that would make sense to them?

4. If a nonbelieving family member or friend was drawing near the end of their life and they asked you, "How can I prepare for eternity and be ready to meet God?" what would you say to them? How would you help them prepare?

> *What Jesus did with his own grave,*
> *he promises to do with yours: empty it.*
>
> —MAX LUCADO

5. **Read:** Luke 18:31–33; 24:45–47. Imagine you were one of the disciples who walked with Jesus and heard him talk about his death and resurrection with such crystal clarity. How could they have heard these words and still not have realized that Jesus was actually going to rise from the dead? Give examples of ways that we hear Jesus declare things with clarity and conviction but still don't fully embrace the truth of what he says.

6. In the video Max talked about how the disciples got stuck on Saturday (Jesus' body in the tomb), but they needed to move into Sunday (Christ risen and alive!). How can Christians today get stuck on Saturday and forget that we live in the glorious victory of Resurrection Sunday? What can we do to inspire ourselves, and others, to live in the hope and reality of Easter Sunday?

7. **Read:** 1 Corinthians 15:12 – 18. Why is absolute confidence in the bodily resurrection of Jesus so critical to the Christian faith? According to the apostle Paul, what are the implications for us if Christ has not risen from the dead?

> *Jesus has risen. Not risen from sleep. Not risen from confusion. Not risen from stupor or slumber. Not spiritually raised from the dead; physically raised. The women and disciples didn't see a phantom or experience a sentiment. They saw Jesus in the flesh.*
>
> —MAX LUCADO

8. **Read:** 1 Corinthians 15:42 – 58. How does the resurrection of Jesus and our assurance of eternal life, through faith in his name, impact our lives today and forever?

9. **Read:** John 11:17 – 27. How does Jesus connect his resurrection and the eternal condition of those who have faith in him? If we

believe these words of Jesus, how should our assurance of eternal life impact the way we live today?

10. When we are assured of Jesus' resurrection and confident that heaven is our home, everything changes. What transformation have you experienced in *one* of these areas as you have grown more and more confident that the final chapter of your life is really just a preface to eternity with God?

- How you view this life and the way you invest your time ...

- How you share God's love and message of grace with others ...

- How you use your resources and the way you view material things ...

- How you view and treat people who have not yet entered a saving relationship with Jesus ...

- Some other area of your life ...

Which one of these areas would you desire to grow in and how can your small group members pray for you as you journey forward?

CLOSING PRAYER

Take time as a group to pray in some of the following directions:

- Thank Jesus for his sacrificial death in your place on the cross ... to deal with all your sins. And thank him for his glorious resurrection and the certainty you have that heaven will be your home because he has opened and prepared the way!

- Pray for people you love and care about who have still not embraced God's plan for their life and eternity.

- Confess where you get stuck on Saturday and forget to celebrate the joy and confidence that result in knowing that Sunday has come and Jesus has risen.

- Ask God to help you walk in the resurrection power of Jesus each and every day of your life.

> *Death is not the final chapter in your story. In death you will step into the arms of the One who declared, "I am the resurrection and the life. He who believes in me will live, even though he dies; and whoever lives and believes in me will never die" (John 11:25–26).*
>
> —MAX LUCADO

BETWEEN SESSIONS

Personal Reflection

Read: 1 Corinthians 15. Reflect on the importance of Jesus' resurrection—to you personally and on a broader level. What would be different if Jesus had not risen? How has hope invaded our world through the resurrection? What do you have to look forward to because Jesus rose from the dead and you have received his grace?

Personal Action

So many people have no "exit strategy" from this world. They are caught up in the distractions and stuff of life and don't think past the next week or month. Commit to pray for family and friends who have not entered a life-saving friendship with Jesus. Ask God to give you opportunities to move from prayer into action as you share with others what the resurrection of Jesus means to you and what it could mean in their life ... and eternity.

Group Engagement

Most communities are home to service and mission organizations that serve meals (or provide other assistance) to the poor. Find a date (either a holiday or maybe a weekend in the near future) where your group could serve together in a local ministry. If you have kids, you might want to invite them to take part. As you prepare to serve and as you engage with people in this time of need, pray for opportunities to share not only your time, food, and service, but also the hope of the resurrected Jesus.

YOU WILL FINALLY GRADUATE

*We cling tightly to this life,
but for followers of Jesus,
the best is yet to come!*

INTRODUCTION

Promises, promises, promises! Advertisers constantly pummel us with pitches that guarantee all sorts of things. Drive this car and your life will shift into a new gear of excitement and meaning. Wear this deodorant and the ladies will flock to you with irresistible passion. Use this weight-loss program and the pounds will melt off in a matter of weeks (and apparently your teeth will become whiter, you'll smile more, and you'll get a new hair style too).

Unfortunately, promises, promises, and more promises often lead to cynicism and skepticism.

The new car does not bring the excitement we expected, but only higher insurance premiums. The deodorant does not make us a magnet for the affection we desire ... it only makes us smell like we are trying a little too hard. The newest weight-loss fad really helps for the first week, and then we look in the mirror to discover that our hips, teeth, and hair look pretty much the same as they did when we started the program.

With the hype of too many promises that fail to deliver, we can become numb to any new promise we hear ... even promises from God. In particular, when we receive assurances of a better world beyond this one, eternal hope, a heavenly home that awaits us, and the promise of a glorious new body, it can all seem too good to be true.

If we are not careful, we can become jaded and cynical ... even when it comes to God's promise of heaven.

> *Heaven has scheduled a graduation. Sin will no longer be at war with our flesh. Eyes won't lust, thoughts won't wander, hands won't steal, our minds won't judge, appetites won't rage, and our tongues won't lie. We will be brand-new.*
>
> —MAX LUCADO

TALK ABOUT IT

Tell about a time you tried a new product with high hopes and expectations only to end up discouraged and disheartened when the advertising promises did not match your reality.

DVD TEACHING NOTES

As you watch the video teaching segment for session 6, featuring Max Lucado, use the following outline to record anything that stands out to you.

Graduation is no small matter

All things in Christ

Sigh of sadness in suffering

Jesus heals

We shall be like Jesus

No more curse

How to live these days on earth

DVD DISCUSSION

1. In the video, Max talked about how the same night became the graduation date of his daughter (from school) and his mother (from this life). How is the day a Christian dies really a graduation day? What are we graduating from and what are we graduating to?

2. **Read:** 1 Corinthians 15:35 – 44. One promise God makes is that when this life ends, we will receive a new and eternal body. How will our new bodies be an upgrade compared to the ones we have right now? What is one thing that excites you about receiving a new body?

3. **Read:** Mark 7:31 – 35. Jesus did a lot of healing while he was on this earth. As you look at this account and others recorded in the four Gospels (Matthew, Mark, Luke, and John), what do you learn about how Jesus healed? What do you learn about why Jesus healed people?

> *I hate disease.*
> *I'm sick of it.*
> *So is Christ.*
> —MAX LUCADO

4. We know that when this life ends and we graduate, we will receive new bodies. Until then, the Bible tells us that we can and should pray for healing for those who are sick and face physical struggles (James 5:13 – 16). Who are you praying for right now and how can your group members join you in both praying for and caring for these people?

5. **Read:** 1 John 3:1–3. What do you learn about God in this passage? What do you learn about yourself?

6. First John 3:2 assures us that one day (postgraduation) "we shall be like [Jesus]." In what ways are we already becoming more like Jesus? In what ways will we be even more like Jesus after our final graduation day? In what ways will Jesus always be unique and different from us?

7. **Read:** Romans 7:15–19. The apostle Paul is brutally honest about the struggle we all face with sin in this life. What does Paul say about our battle with sin and how do his words resonate with your experience?

8. In light of what the apostle Paul teaches in Romans 7, what is one thing you really want to do, but find it difficult to follow through on?

What is one thing you find yourself doing, but you hate it and want to stop? How can your group pray for you and keep you accountable in these areas of your life?

9. **Read:** Revelation 22:1–3. After our graduation day, the curse of sin will be gone. How does this promise give hope in this life? What are some sins and struggles that you look forward to dismissing?

10. **Read:** 2 Corinthians 4:16–18 and Romans 8:18. How does the apostle Paul compare this life to the life to come? How can a passage like this help us when we face pain, struggles, and loss?

Why is meditating on heaven and remembering what comes after graduation day so important for Christians?

CLOSING PRAYER

Take time as a group to pray in some of the following directions:

- Thank God that heaven really is your home and that Jesus has already gone ahead of you to prepare the way.

- Tell God of your heartache concerning the pain and struggles of this world. Pray for his compassion to fill your heart so that you can help bring his grace, love, and comfort to those who are hurting.

- Lift up people you care about who are facing physical ailments and challenges. Ask for the grace of God, his comfort, and his healing touch to be upon them.

- Thank God for the people you love who have gone before you to heaven. Praise God that they were part of your life for a season and that they are with Jesus now.

> *Some of you indwell such road-weary bodies: knees ache, eyes dim, skin sags. Others exited the womb on an uphill ride. While I have no easy answers for your struggle, I implore you to see your challenge in the scope of God's story. View these days on earth as but the opening lines of his sweeping saga.*
>
> —MAX LUCADO

IN THE COMING DAYS

Personal Reflection

One day the curse of sin will be gone (Revelation 22:3), but until our final graduation we will do battle with it. This week identify two or three areas of temptation with which the Enemy tries to lure you. Then do three things: (1) pray for eyes to see and power to overcome the tactics of the Enemy; (2) take practical steps to avoid places and situations that would open the door to possible temptation in these areas of struggle; (3) invite a trusted member of your small group to pray for you and keep you accountable to walk in holiness in these areas.

Personal Action

Make a list of people you care about who are dealing with physical ailments and ongoing health issues. Commit to pray for them on a weekly basis. As circumstances permit, give them an occasional call and pray with them over the phone, or meet with them for prayer. When God answers prayers for healing, praise him and give him the glory. When there is no healing, continue praying and place your trust in God's sovereign power and wisdom.

Group Engagement

As you wrap up this study, consider a next step you can take together as a group.

SMALL GROUP LEADER HELPS

To ensure a successful small group experience, read the following information before beginning.

GROUP PREPARATION

Whether your small group has been meeting together for years or is gathering for the first time, be sure to designate a consistent time and place to work through the six sessions. Once you establish the when and where of your times together, select a facilitator who will keep discussions on track and an eye on the clock. If you choose to rotate this responsibility, assign the six sessions to their respective facilitators upfront, so that group members can prepare their thoughts and questions prior to the session they are responsible for leading. Follow the same assignment procedure should your group want to serve any snacks/beverages.

A NOTE TO FACILITATORS

As facilitator, you are responsible for honoring the agreed-upon timeframe of each meeting, for prompting helpful discussion among your group, and for keeping the dialogue equitable by drawing out quieter members and helping more talkative members to remember that others' insights are valued in your group.

You might find it helpful to preview each session's video teaching segment and then scan the "DVD Discussion" questions that pertain to it, highlighting various questions that you want to be sure to cover during your group's meeting. Ask God in advance of your time together to guide your group's discussion, and then be sensitive to the direction he wishes to lead.

Urge participants to bring their participant's guide, pen, and a Bible to every gathering.

SESSION FORMAT

Each session of the participant's guide includes the following group components:

- **"Introduction"** — an entrée to the session's topic, which may be read by a volunteer or summarized by the facilitator
- **"Talk About It"** — an icebreaker question that relates to the session topic and invites input from every group member
- **"DVD Teaching Notes"** — an outline of the session's 10 – 12 minute video teaching for group members to follow along and take notes if they wish
- **"DVD Discussion"** — video-related and Bible exploration questions that reinforce the session content and elicit personal input from every group member
- **"Closing Prayer"** — several prayer cues to guide group members in closing prayer

Additionally, in each session you will find a **"Between Sessions"** section that includes suggestions for personal and group response.

9780849947483

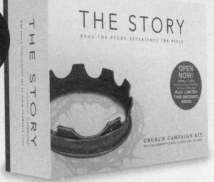

BOOKS AND CURRICULUM FOR ALL AGES
PERFECT FOR SUNDAY SCHOOL AND SMALL GROUPS

ADULT CURRICULUM

Adult curriculum helps small groups of any form or size learn, discuss, and apply the themes in The Heart of the Story. Designed to be used independently or as part of The Story 31-week campaign.

TEEN CURRICULUM

Experiential learning and fun; creative; best-in-class HD video and lesson plans help teens clearly understand *The Story*.

CHILDREN'S BOOKS AND CURRICULUM

Three new children's books, including *The Story for Children* by Max Lucado, help bring the Bible to life for readers of any age. Reproducible lesson plans make for easy implementation in children's programs.

To order visit www.TheStory.com

THE STORY
POWERED BY ZONDERVAN

MUSIC INSPIRED BY

THE STORY

THE STORY is an unparalleled CD & DVD project from the best-known artists in Christian music. The songs on THE STORY take timeless biblical stories and provide a completely new context into how God's story of *love & redemption* intersects with our story of *brokenness & failures* resulting in a new story of *hope and rescue*. The CD contains 18 songs while the DVD includes all-new dramatic film footage of each character and song on THE STORY. As you listen, you will gain new insight into timeless biblical stories and rediscover how God's story becomes *yours*.

INCLUDES PERFORMANCES BY:

FRANCESCA BATTISTELLI
BLANCA CALLAHAN
from GROUP 1 CREW
JEREMY CAMP
STEVEN CURTIS CHAPMAN
PETER FURLER
AMY GRANT
NATALIE GRANT
MARK HALL & MEGAN GARRETT
from CASTING CROWNS

MATT HAMMITT
from SANCTUS REAL
DAN HASELTINE
from JARS OF CLAY
BRANDON HEATH
MANDISA
BART MILLARD
from MERCY ME
LECRAE
LEIGH NASH

NICHOLE NORDEMAN
MAC POWELL
from THIRD DAY
MICHAEL W. SMITH
TODD SMITH
from SELAH
MICHAEL TAIT
from NEWSBOYS
CHRIS TOMLIN
MATTHEW WEST

World Vision and THE STORY partners have joined together to give a portion of proceeds from The Story CD to help provide life in all its fullness for those in need. For more information on World Vision and how you can make a difference around the world, visit *www.worldvision.org*.

IN PARTNERSHIP WITH

   ZONDERVAN

TheStoryCD.com
TheStoryDVD.com